THE LIFE BOOK OF CHRISTMAS · VOLUME THREE

# THE MERRIMENT OF CHRISTMAS

BY THE EDITORS OF

**LIFE**

A
STONEHENGE
BOOK

TIME INCORPORATED, NEW YORK

TIME INC. BOOK DIVISION

*Editor*  Norman P. Ross

*Copy Director* William Jay Gold  *Art Director* Edward A. Hamilton

*Chief of Research*  Beatrice T. Dobie

Editorial staff for Volume Three of
THE LIFE BOOK OF CHRISTMAS

*Editor*  Stanley Fillmore

*Designer*  Norman Snyder

*Text*  Neal G. Stuart (Chief), John Stanton,
Barbara Elias, Jean T. Freeman,
Jonathan Kastner, Edmund White

*Chief Researcher*  Carlotta Kerwin

*Researchers*  Jeanne S. Dempsey, Audrey Foote,
Mary Ellen Murphy, Kaye Neil, Donald Nelson,
Jenifer Ratliff, Jean Sulzberger

*Picture Researchers*  Margaret K. Goldsmith, Joan T. Lynch

*Art Associate*  Robert L. Young

*Art Assistants*  James D. Smith, John Newcomb,
Robert McElrath, David Wyland

*Copy Staff*  Marian Gordon Goldman,
Rosalind Stubenberg, Dolores A. Littles

*Publisher*  Jerome S. Hardy

*General Manager*  John A. Watters

LIFE MAGAZINE

*Editor*  Edward K. Thompson

*Managing Editor*  George P. Hunt

*Publisher*  C. D. Jackson

The following individuals and departments of Time
Inc. helped in producing this book: Doris O'Neil, Chief
of the LIFE Picture Library; Content Peckham, Chief
of the Time Inc. Bureau of Editorial Reference;
Donald Bermingham and Clara Applegate of the
TIME-LIFE News Service; and Correspondents Gerda
Endler (Bonn), Katharine Sachs (London), Piero
Saporiti (Madrid), Page d'Aulnay (Paris) and Ger-
traud Lessing (Vienna).

# CONTENTS
## VOLUME THREE

# INTRODUCTION

It was a 15th Century follower of St. Francis of Assisi who wrote, "Nowe let us syng and mery be For Crist oure kyng hathe set us fre." Another Franciscan carol in the same vein exults: "O, my heart is full of mirth At Jesus' birth."

It was this merry rejoicing at Christ's birth which inspired, in parts of medieval England, Scotland and Ireland, the annual celebration of "the devil's funeral." For an hour before midnight on Christmas Eve, the village churchbells tolled slowly and mournfully. Then, just at midnight, the belfries rang out a paean of joy and deliverance—for it was believed that the devil died when Jesus Christ was born.

Today bells and carillons still call men to rejoice on Christmas Day. The shout of "Merry Christmas!" rings through the holidays along with the mere solemn refrain of that first Christmas: peace on earth. The evergreen tree glowing with ornaments, the wreath on the door, the turkey in the oven, stockings hung above the fireplace, carols sung in snowy streets—all express the merriment of this most festive season.

Volume Three of THE LIFE BOOK OF CHRISTMAS seeks to capture the warmth, good will and inventive zest that make up the Christmas spirit today; Volume One goes back to the source of that spirit, the glory and wonder of the first Christmas; and Volume Two describes the growing enrichment of Christmas through the ages and in many lands.

As explained in Volume Two, Christmas decorations date from ancient times and come from many places. The exquisite cathedral collage *(opposite)* was inspired by medieval illumination but was actually constructed by an imaginative modern artist out of bits of wrapping paper and Christmas seals.

Chapter I presents a wealth of such ingenious decorating ideas. The elaborate but edible gingerbread house, the bright felt wall hanging, the paper figures for the Twelve Days of Christmas, the Della Robbia wreath, all are based on traditional decorating themes, but were created especially for this book by artists who carefully designed them so they could be made by amateurs.

Chapter II traces the tradition of holiday hospitality down through the years. The recipes given here— all of ancient lineage but adapted for modern cooks—include unusual suggestions for parties as well as for the family Christmas dinner, and an imaginative assortment of drinks and punches derived from the convivial wassail bowl.

Fun for children is the theme of Chapter III. Here are lively games to play, a fascinating puzzle based on a 16th Century painting, and a play children can produce themselves for the entertainment of the family.

At the end of each chapter, an anthology of poems, stories and songs comments further on the subject. The final photographic essay expresses the special magic of Christmas as it is newly created each season.

According to Proverbs, "A merry heart maketh a cheerful countenance." The aim of this book is to make the heart merry and thus to add to the merriment of Christmas.

—THE EDITORS OF LIFE

# I
# FAMILY DECORATIONS

DEEP IN THE WINTER NIGHT, the family will come one by one, carrying great and small boxes, brilliant in all colors, ribboned in red and green, silver and gold, bright blue, placing them under me with the hands of their hearts, until all around me they are piled high, climbing up into my branches, spilling over onto the floor about me. In the early morning, with all my candles burning and all my brilliant colors standing out and twinkling in their light, the children in their pajamas and woolen slippers rub their sleeping eyes and stare at me in amazement. The mother with her hair hanging down her back smiles and glances here and there, and the father looks up and down at me, quiet and pleased...for I am the Christmas tree.

"THE BOOK OF THE YEAR," FRITZ PETERS

*"GOD BLESS US, every one," is the sentiment lettered over the arch in this elaborately decorated 19th Century dining room (opposite).*

# MAKING YOUR HOUSE SHOUT, "CHRISTMAS!"

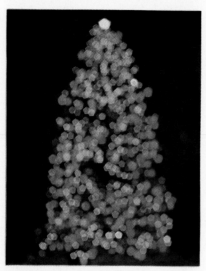

IN MULTICOLORED GLORY, *a 67-foot tree stands in Rockefeller Plaza, New York. It typifies community trees across the nation.*

"GET IVYE and hull [holly] woman deck up thine house," advised Thomas Tusser in the 16th Century. At times of great joy and celebration, man seems naturally to turn to boughs and branches to decorate home and church. The oak, holly and the "golden bough," thought to be mistletoe, were sacred to the Romans, and flowers as well as greenery are part of the Jewish Feast of Tabernacles. Jesus, entering triumphantly into Jerusalem, was praised with palms.

So it is that the great celebration of Christmas inspires the most extravagant decorations. The world proclaims the merry season as houses are decked with holly and pine, with mistletoe and poinsettia—and most important of all, with the family Christmas tree.

Americans decorate nearly 40 million of them every year. They start moving to markets in November—mostly five- to eight-year-old bushy balsams and Douglas firs, but also spruces, cedars, pines and hemlocks. Few decisions a family may make in a year are likely to receive so much loving consideration and passionate debate as the purchase and decoration of the tree. Once chosen and set up, the family star is ceremoniously placed on top. Next come the strings of lights, and they are certain to set off argument over whether there are too many green lights on one side and not enough blue on the other. Then come gleaming balls in brilliant colors and the gay frivolities—the bells, lanterns, cones, reflectors and icicles, and the paper chains pasted and popcorn strung by the children. Every family divides on the issue of the final tinsel. Elders hang it strand by strand, while younger members take delight in tossing it by the handful.

How all this trimming of trees began no one really knows. It is said that Hessian soldiers serving with the British during the American Revolution made Christmas trees popular in America. In Europe, credit for beginning them is sometimes given to the Reformation leader Martin Luther, who, walking home one clear winter's night, saw the stars twinkling through the evergreen trees. To show his family the loveliness he had seen, he erected a tree in his house and set candles agleam on its branches. But others date Christmas trees back farther, to the "paradise trees" of the Christmas morality plays in Germany during the Middle Ages. They were hung with apples, to tempt Adam and Eve, and wafers, to symbolize the Eucharist. Eventually people began setting up the trees in their homes.

Soon the joyful spirit of the celebration added other things to the apples on the trees: little baked stars, angels and hearts. The custom (still observed in Ireland and eastern Europe) of relighting one big candle every night during Christmas to symbolize God's presence on earth grew to include smaller candles arranged on little wooden pyramids. By the 18th Century the candles had been transferred to the Christmas tree itself, and clever little holders, shaped like tiny fish or hands, were designed to hold them steady while the tiny flames danced and flickered among the branches. Four hundred candles were considered sufficient for a 12-foot tree, while pails of water and servants holding long wet mops were kept ready in case of emergency.

The appearance of strings of colored electric lights in 1907 banished these dangers, save in northern Europe where some families cling to candles even today and make Christmas Eve the fireman's busiest night. In 1909, with all-weather wiring, Pasadena, California, started the American custom of community Christmas trees by lighting one atop Mount Wilson overlooking the city. Cleveland, Ohio, and New York City followed suit in 1912. Now, aside from the National Christmas Tree on the White House lawn, perhaps the most famous of the great outdoor trees is the one decorated annually in Rockefeller Plaza, New York (left, above), visited each year by more than two and a half million people. As every city and town took advantage of the new wiring, entire streets and shopping areas became ablaze with lights.

By the early 1930s outdoor lights came to the homes, setting streets and country lanes sparkling with the holiday spirit. Now doorways gleam in multicolored lights, trees on lawns blossom in red, green, yellow, orange and blue. Roofs, chimneys and even entire houses are outlined in Christmas lights. Indoors and out, decorations call out everyone's wishes for the merriest of Christmases.

THE FAMILY TREE *stands at the center of Christmas, transforming the living room with its splendid size and fragrance. All the ceremonies around it—the shopping together for one of just the right size and fullness, the trimming of its branches with ornaments cherished down the years, and the excited opening of presents on Christmas morning—serve to unite the family.*

STAINED-GLASS STARS *recall the patterns of crystal hoarfrost on the pane. Designs are easy to transfer to windows. (Instructions page 28.)*

# NEW FORMS
# FOR THE
# CHRISTMAS STAR

One of the universal beliefs of man is that great events on earth should be accompanied by startling phenomena in the sky; movements of the heavenly bodies, in Shakespeare's phrase, are "harbingers preceding still the fates."

The light that led the Wise Men to Bethlehem was such a phenomenon, yet in the Christian tradition the star is associated with more than the Nativity. Mary is sometimes honored as *Stella Maris*—Star of the Sea—and Christ said, "I am the root and the offspring of David, and the bright and morning star."

The star has long been an integral part of Christmas. In many parts of Europe, bands of "star singers" still carry poles topped with star-shaped lanterns and go through the streets singing carols on Christmas Eve. Wherever trees are decked, the star is a favorite choice for the top.

WITH A TOUCH OF MAGIC *such simple household articles as toothpicks and straws are converted into a shimmering constellation. (Instructions page 28.)*

SWEDISH WALL HANGING *from 1839 is titled "Jesus and His parents resting during their journey." It is in the Nordic Museum in Stockholm.*

## WARM COLORS FOR WALLS

In medieval Scandinavia, Christmas was heralded in peasant homes by the "drawing" of the cottage. Bare walls of unpainted timber or white-washed clay were brought alive with home-spun tapestries of Nativity and other Biblical scenes. Colors were bright and figures were primitive, but the designs often had great ingenuity and humor.

This tradition of special wall hangings in simple homes had its roots in pre-Christian days, but the idea was readily adaptable to Christmas celebrations and probably borrowed further from church tapestries.

Gradually the work of weaving an entire tapestry was simplified; people began painting the scenes directly onto cloth or paper. By the middle of the 19th Century, the painting of wall hangings had all but ceased, though the custom still lingers in Christmas prints for hanging that may be bought in Swedish stores. Families that have managed to preserve old wall hangings still display them at Christmastime. The end of the Swedish Christmas season comes on January 13, St. Knut's Day. The children have a final party, and the hangings are taken down and stored until next year.

MODERN VERSION *of a wall hanging is this one in bright felt of the Three Wise Men bearing their gifts to the Child. Faces, robes and vessels for the gifts are traditional, yet the stylized lines make the hanging contemporary. (Instructions page 29.)*

GRIMM'S ENCHANTED HOUSE, *spirited from its fabled German forest, provides a fairy-tale touch for Christmas. But it runs the risk of being nibbled by children. (Instructions page 30.)*

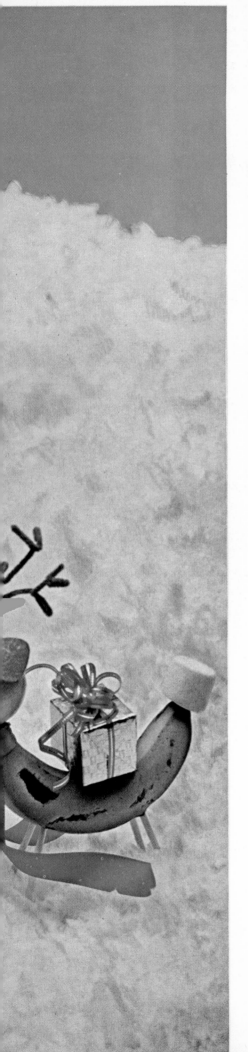

# FANTASIES FOR THE LIVING ROOM

" 'We will set to work on that,' said Hänsel, 'and have a good meal. I will eat a bit of the roof, and you Gretel, can eat some of the window, it will taste sweet.' " The children in Jakob Grimm's famous fairy tale promptly started devouring the witch's gingerbread house, until they were interrupted by a voice issuing from the parlor: " 'Nibble, nibble, gnaw, Who is nibbling at my little house?' " The children answered: " 'The wind.' " Although gingerbread has been baked since ancient times, and tales of gingerbread figures are numerous, it was Grimm (1785-1863) who started the tradition of baking gay gingerbread houses at Christmas. Perhaps the fact that his was occupied by a child-eating witch has made the decoration seem exciting and enchanted, but also slightly evil, just as gingerbread itself is sweet at first bite, but leaves a spicy aftertaste. However, other associations with gingerbread are pleasanter. "And may your happiness ever spread Like butter on hot gingerbread," an old couplet reads.

FRUIT AND CANDY CHARACTERS, *put together with toothpicks and imagination, parade across the snow. Delectably alive, they are to be admired, not eaten. (Instructions page 29.)*

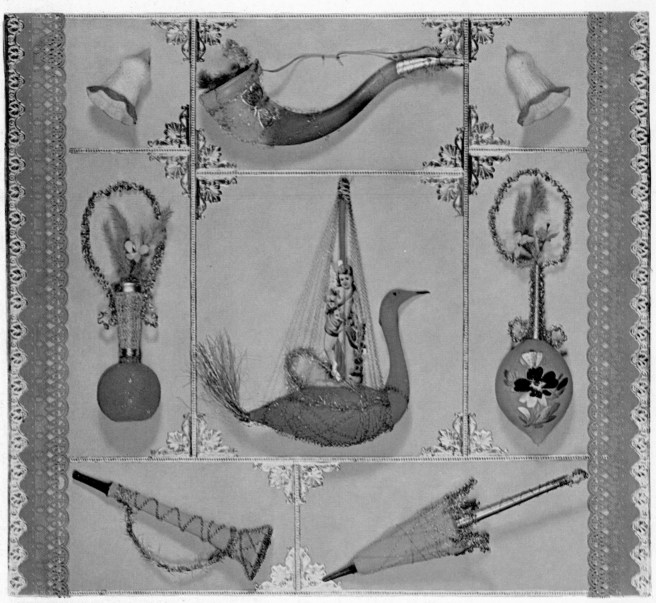

ORNAMENTS OF THE PAST *are recalled by these German decorations dating from before World War I. The colors used were those of earlier confectioners' delights in sugar which once hung from every tree. The ornate bird with the spun-glass tail was a particularly popular decoration of the era.*

# TREE ORNAMENTS OLD AND NEW

Trimming a tree with ornaments is a tradition that comes from ancient Rome, but Christmas tree decorations as such have come to us from 16th Century Germany. There, trees were hung with gilded nuts, apples, sugar figures, dolls and shepherds. Queen Victoria's German husband, Prince Albert, introduced the custom to England. In 1841 the royal family celebrated the holidays around a gigantic tree covered with wax tapers and sweetmeats.

Not until 1860 did glass trinkets begin to replace edible ornaments. Again the Germans took the lead; peasants in central Germany worked at the primitive industry in their cottages. The father blew the glass figures, the rest of the family painted them with fancy designs.

Today's tree may be less mouthwatering than those once trimmed with sweets, but permanent ornaments have one advantage: around a familiar star or angel, a family can each year build up its own traditions.

ORNAMENTS OF TODAY, *in contrast to the elaborate ones of old, are usually simply designed. These paper cutouts are remarkably easy to make, yet look sophisticated. (Instructions page 30.)*

# THE TWELVE DAYS OF CHRISTMAS

"The twelfth day of Christmas
My true love sent to me:
Twelve ladies dancing,
Eleven lords a-leaping,
Ten drummers drumming,
Nine pipers piping,
Eight maids a-milking,
Seven swans a-swimming,
Six geese a-laying

Five gold rings;
Four colly birds,
Three French hens,
Two turtle doves,
And a partridge in pear tree."
The imaginative true love sent, in all, 78 gifts on the 12th day alone. The colorful paper version above might decorate the Christmas dinner

20

table, the mantelpiece or any generous-sized area where a festive note is wanted. The song itself has its origins in a game still played in England. Players suggest nonsensical, tongue-twisting gifts in turn, but after adding to it, each must repeat the ever-lengthening list in full. The first to make a slip or forget one of the absurd gifts surrenders a forfeit.

The 12 days begin on Christmas Day and end on January 6—Epiphany, or Twelfth Night, when the Three Wise Men came with their gifts for the Christ Child. Twelfth Night in England had many pagan overtones and was traditionally celebrated with masquerading, dancing and merrymaking—a final fling before the seasonal fun was over. Traditionalists today still wait until Twelfth Night to dismantle the tree. Some towns now celebrate with a neighborhood tree-burning bonfire, after which everyone troops to someone's home for a modern wassail: hot cocoa. (Instructions pages 31-32.)

WREATHED BY FRUITS, *the Madonna adores the Babe in this terra-cotta relief from the Italian Renaissance workshop of the Della Robbia family. She is joined by an ox, ass and cherubim.*

# THE CROWNING WREATH

The wreath has a long history and many religious associations. In classical times the winner of an athletic contest was crowned with a laurel wreath. The less worldly Christians made the wreath a symbol of a more enduring victory—Christ's conquest over death and the forces of darkness. Perhaps the loveliest use of this symbol is the Advent wreath. In many European homes, on each of the four Sundays before Christmas, one of the four candles on the wreath is lighted and prayers are said in anticipation of the holy event.

In northern countries wreaths are usually made of evergreen, but in a Mediterranean land like Italy it is not unusual to discover garlands of fruit woven into holiday decorations. The Della Robbia family, a succession of Renaissance Florentine artists famous for their enameled terra-cotta work, included in their sculptured wreaths oranges, pears, cucumbers, apples, chestnuts, poppies, pine cones and grapes. Northern pine sprays set off with a red bow summon up the vision of winter snows and crackling fires. By contrast, the Italian cornucopia of fruits and vegetables evokes the image of a softer, balmier season—which is, after all, closer to the first Christmas.

THE ANCIENT SHAPE *is described with modern materials—aluminum foil and water-repellent ribbon. (Instructions page 33.)*

A MODERN "DELLA ROBBIA" WREATH *combines northern evergreens and Mediterranean and other fruits—a blending that is characteristic of a new tradition arising from older ones. The pleasant custom of the wreath on the front door is American. (Instructions page 33.)*

23

STEALING A KISS *under the mistletoe is a custom that comes from England. "Turn where you will," wrote Erasmus of that country in the 16th Century, "there are kisses, kisses everywhere."*

# EVERGREEN
# WITH
# A DIFFERENCE

For thousands of years, evergreens have been a symbol of indestructible life in the midst of winter desolation. Long before Christ, people of the chilly north took greenery into their homes as reassurance that life endured.

Because of their apparently supernatural ability to withstand the winter, legends sprang up around them. Mistletoe was sacred to England's druids. Priests in ceremonial white robes climbed trees to cut the parasitic evergreen with sickles of gold.

Holly, whose red berries symbolize Christ's blood and sharp thorns His hurtful crown, is hung to bring luck to the home and as an invitation to the spirit of the Christ child to enter. An old English tale declares that, for the sake of marital harmony within the home, "He-holly, that with prickles on its leaves, must not be brought into the house before the She-holly, that with the smooth-edged leaves." The two sexes must enter together.

24

THE ESPALIER TREE *of perfect symmetry recalls fruit trees of European gardens, trained against sunny walls. (Instructions page 34.)*

PRECURSOR TO THE CHRISTMAS TREE *is this German decoration of a pyramid of greenery decked with fruit. (Instructions page 34.)*

THE FESTOON OF EVERGREEN *goes back to Greco-Roman days. Hung with red ribbons, pine cones and holly, this graceful curve is frequently used in churches. (Instructions page 34.)*

25

CHRISTMAS WRAPPINGS, *once used simply to disguise the present, are today an integral part of the gift itself. With such a rich assortment of colored papers, foil, bright ribbons and decorative tape available, even the wrapper with all thumbs becomes an artist. (Instructions pages 35-37.)*

# PACKAGES AND PINATAS

Christmas would be a lot simpler if presents came in brown paper sacks, but as long as the spirit abides, families will stay up till the small hours of Christmas Eve tying bows and wrapping their love in tissue paper. The cause is well worth the trouble. One of the most glorious moments of Christmas Day is its beginning, when all the mystery and the promise of the season seem to be contained in the still unopened, beautifully wrapped gifts under the tree.

Giving presents around the new year started long before Christianity. The Romans had the charming habit of distributing symbolic gifts among friends: honeyed things, to bring sweetness in the coming year; lamps, to ensure light and warmth; and small presents of gold and silver, to bestow increasing wealth on the recipient. In the Christian tradition, the first and most splendid bearers of gifts were the Magi, who offered precious things in rich ves-

sels to the little boy in the manger.

In Mexico, the piñata is a curious, playful receptacle for presents. On Christmas Eve, children are blindfolded and given sticks. Each child attempts to strike and break open the piñata, which is a clay jar decorated to look like an animal, a doll, even an airplane. When the fortunate contestant smashes the jar, its contents—candy, fruits, sweetmeats and nuts—come showering to the ground for everyone to grab.

BOBBING MERRILY, *an elf is thwacked by blindfolded, excited children. Sooner or later a well-aimed blow will break the piñata and spill forth its cache of candies. (Instructions page 37.)*

26

# STARS

## STAINED GLASS WINDOW

*Photograph on page 12*

*Medium bottle
of clear glue (mucilage)
Food coloring
Tracing paper
Cellophane tape
Watercolor brush; small bowl*

Clean window. Draw design on tracing paper. Tape paper to outside of window. For each different color required, pour about a tablespoon of mucilage into small bowl and add about six drops of one color or combination of colors. Test on window for deepness of color. Paint all areas calling for this color, then mix second color. When painting, separate colors by about ¼" to prevent them from running and to simulate the leading of real stained glass windows. Spread newspaper beneath the window to catch drippings. A damp cloth will help correct mistakes, and paint may be removed with a wet cloth even after it has dried.

*each square equals 2"*

## TOOTHPICK STAR

*Photograph on page 13*

*One styrofoam ball,
1" in diameter
One box plastic toothpicks*

Stick all the toothpicks in the ball as shown, forming rays. To hang, tie a thread to one of the toothpicks (make sure it is driven in securely), or to a straight pin stuck in the ball.

## SODA STRAW STAR

*Photograph on page 13*

*75 paper or cellophane soda
straws, 15 of them
cut in half
Crochet cord
Piece of florist's wire, a
bit more than twice
as long as a soda straw,
for a needle*

Straw stars are built around a core, which itself is a series of triangles. Straws are threaded together with crochet cord, using a needle of florist's wire. Though held together only by cord, they are well braced by the triangular construction, and the stars are not fragile. To make needle, bend wire double, making a loop narrow enough to pass through a straw (A). To make the core, pass needle and thread through three of the half-straws, draw them into a triangle, cut cord and tie ends together. To attach a second triangle to first, pass the needle again through one of the half-straws of the first triangle, then through two other half-straws, cut cord and tie. Make four joined triangles in this way, then link bases of first and fourth triangles with one half-straw and tie cord ends tightly (B). This is the top of the core, which now looks like (C). Thread additional triangles around the sides (D). Add five more triangles around the bottom to form a reverse pyramid exactly like the top one (E), using up all half-straws, and the core is done. For points of star, full-length straws are used, three to a point. Each of the 20 triangles of the core is the base for a star point. To make each point, thread needle first through a base straw, then upward through a long straw, down through a second long straw, leading thread back to starting point. Without cutting, thread through second base straw, up through a third long straw, down again through second long straw to starting point (F). Cut and tie. Continue this process for all 20 points. The blue star on page 13 looks much more complex than the other two, but it is not more difficult to make. Two points instead of one are attached to each base triangle, one made of full-length straws and the other of half-straws (G). To make this double-pointed star, 60 additional half-straws will be needed; attach a point made of half-straws to one of the core triangles, then attach a point made of full-length straws to the same triangle; continue thus around the core.

A

B

C

D

E

F

G

28

# WALL HANGING

## FELT TAPESTRY OF THREE WISE MEN

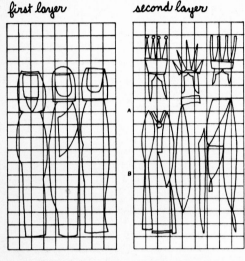

first layer

second layer

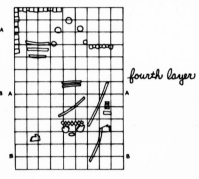

third layer

each square equals 2"

fourth layer

*Photograph on page 15*

*Tan felt 3' x 1½' for background*
*Three 3' x 9" pieces of lightweight felt for robes: orange, white and purple*
*Small squares of felt for details in colors indicated in photograph*
*Casein glue, white chalk, scissors, single-edged razor blade*
*Tracing or tissue paper*

Original designs of felt on felt are simply made. To duplicate Three Wise Men, diagrams at left illustrate the successive layers of felt to be added to the background. Expand each item in drawings to scale on tracing or tissue paper. Transfer each paper drawing onto appropriately colored felt as follows; draw over lines with chalk. Place paper on felt, face down. Trace over lines with pencil on reverse side, lift paper—chalk marks will have transferred to felt. Cut with razor along marks. Do not draw directly on felt. If felt creases or curls at edges, iron smooth. Apply casein glue lightly to back of each cutout: leave ½" border around edges free of glue. If glue should seep beyond edges, scoop it back under with toothpick. Add border of ¾" squares of felt cut from many-colored scraps. When completed, entire tapestry may be ironed.

# EDIBLE ORNAMENTS

## FRUIT FIGURES

*Photograph on page 16*

reindeer

Wise Man

*Variety of fresh fruit as indicated below:*
*Little marshmallows*
*Gumdrops*
*Small candies or raisins*
*Candy-coated chocolate drops*
*Ribbon, gold paper trim*
*Cotton*
*Holly or evergreen*
*Small matchboxes*
*Thread*
*Paper cup*
*Small styrofoam balls*
*8 pipe cleaners*
*Yarn (or raffia)*
*Feathers*
*Toothpicks, wooden skewers and glue*

*Reindeer:* For each antler, twist 2 green pipe cleaners together. Separate other ends and twist in jagged pattern. Insert each antler into lime head. Stick lime on green banana (yellow banana is too soft) with toothpick. Legs are skewers. They should be pointed at one end. Glue on small candies as eyes and nose. Ears are gumdrops attached with toothpicks. Tie ribbon around neck.

*Three Wise Men:* Make head of peach or small apple or orange and attach with toothpick to apple body. Glue circlets of gold trim around heads and bodies as crowns and belts. Arms are skewers with hands of styrofoam balls. Glue on bits of cotton for mustaches and beards. Add eyes and noses of colored pins or raisins. Wrap matchboxes for gifts. Stick sprig of holly or piece of evergreen in one hand, suspend a package on thread from other hand.

*Santa:* Grapefruit body, peach or orange head. Hat is paper cup covered with red paper. Use cotton for mustache and beard, and for trim on hat and body.

*Lady and Man:* Pear body, peach or lemon head, pipe cleaner arms akimbo. Make lady's muff of two marshmallows, man's hands of styrofoam balls. Man's hat is marshmallow decorated with paper fringe. Glue small cookie to lady's head, glue decorations on top. She has white yarn hair. Use velvet ribbons for scarves.

*Girl with Pigtails:* Grapefruit body, orange head. Hair is braided raffia or yarn, glued on. Devise neckpiece of feathery pastel powder puff.

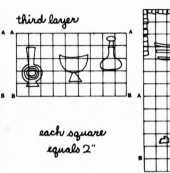

Santa

lady

man

girl with pigtails

## GINGERBREAD HOUSE

*Photograph on page 17*

**Gingersnap dough:**
*1 ½ cups heavy cream*
*2 ½ cups brown sugar*
*¼ cup molasses*
*1 tablespoon ginger*
*2 tablespoons baking soda*
*9 cups all-purpose flour*
*Cardboard*
*Frosting*

Whip cream until very thick, but not stiff, stir in sugar, molasses, ginger and baking soda. Mix until sugar is dissolved. Add flour and work in until smooth, cover and let stand overnight in a cool place (not refrigerator). Cut out five patterns at left in cardboard or construction paper: (A) front and back of house, (B) sides, (C) roof, (D) two sides of chimney, (E) the other two sides of chimney. Put aside ¼ of cookie dough and divide the remaining dough in half. Roll out each half on greased cookie sheet. Lay cardboard patterns on dough. Cut around patterns with sharp knife. Make 2 dough shapes for each pattern; you will have 10 dough shapes altogether. Pull away strips of dough left between sections after cutting. Cut out windows and doors freehand. For an elaborate house, reroll bits of cutaway dough and cut out doors, shutters, stepping stones, fence posts, etc. Bake house sections in a slow oven (300°) about 12 to 15 minutes. Cool on cookie sheet, then remove with broad spatula to rack until ready to assemble. Frosting is used as mortar to join various sections; press sections and frosting together until they hold. Construct and decorate walls, then add roof and chimney. When house is firm, roof may be decorated with animal cutouts made from the remaining ¼ of the original gingersnap dough. Fix animals to house with frosting.

# PAPER ORNAMENTS

## CUTOUTS FOR THE TREE

*Photograph on page 19*

*Sheets of colored paper*
*Paper punch*
*Rubber cement*
*Paper clips*
*Legal seals (from stationer's)*
*Small shiny stars*
*White paper doilies*

Ornaments (A) to (L) each require four 4" x 6" pieces of colored paper. Fold each sheet lengthwise into quarters, forming loosely open hollow square. Stand 4 sheets upright in two rows of two, middle quarters back to back. Glue backs together. When dry, flatten sheets. Construct 12 of these sheets. Cut patterns (A) to (L), one to a set, cutting through all 4 thicknesses of paper at once. Fold back cut sections. Decorate (A) with legal seals; place green stars on seals. Decorate (B) with circles from doilies dotted with red stars. Back doilies with red paper for cutouts on (D). Place red stars in center of flowers of (E). Vary decorations to your taste. Hang on tree with paper clips. Ornaments (M) through (Q) require only one 4" x 6" sheet of paper each. Paper may be colored on one or both sides. Measure length of sheet into quarters with pencil. All cutting must be made in two middle quarters, so it should be done with razor blade. Draw patterns (M) to (Q) with pencil, then cut along those lines. For ornament (O), fold every other section in the opposite direction. Decorate (M) with paper-punch dots. All one-piece ornaments are fastened in back with glue or paper clip. Ornaments (M), (P) and (Q) are circles. Crease (N) to make half-circle, (O) to make triangle.

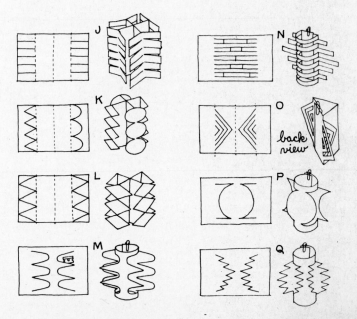

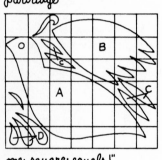

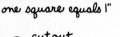

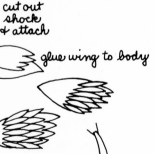

## THE TWELVE DAYS OF CHRISTMAS

Photograph on pages 20-21

*60 cone-shaped paper cups*
*1 plastic beach ball, or styrofoam cut in sphere*
*12" in diameter*
*1 empty oatmeal box (or salt box or mailing tube)*
*50 Ping-pong balls*
*Wrapping-weight papers; dark brown, gold, orange,*
*black, white and any 5 other bright solids; mottled for*
*partridge and French hens; at least 6 gay*
*multicolored patterns for clothing, drum-top*
*Tissue papers: 3 bright colors in small amounts*
*for feathers, tassels, hair, etc.*
*Small paper doilies*
*Paper napkins*
*Toothpicks*
*Black poster paint and*
*small brush*
*Razor, scissors*
*Transparent tape*
*Tweezers*
*Glue*

### 1. Pear Tree

Cut off top of any cylindrical cardboard carton approximately 3" x 5" in diameter and about 8" high. Cover outside with dark brown paper, using glue or tape. Stand cylinder upright and balance ball on open end.

*Leaves:* Fold a sheet of gold paper in half 3 times. Cut from folded sheet oval-shaped leaf about 3½" long from tip to stem. You will be cutting 8 leaves at a time. Altogether, about 125 leaves will be needed to cover tree top. *Pears:* Draw two tangent circles on the reverse side of a sheet of orange paper, using pencil compass or small jar lids. One should be about 1¾" in diameter, the other 1". Draw lines that curve out from either side of the smaller circle to either side of larger circle. Cut out pear shape. Make 8 pears in all.

*Pear stems:* Slender, slightly curving strips of gold paper about ¾" long. Glue or tape to back of pear.

*Application of leaves and pears to tree top:* Form cluster of 6 leaves and attach stems to tree top with glue or 2-sided tape (adhesive on both sides). Now add single leaves in ever-widening ring around original cluster, tucking and gluing stems under leaves already down. After covering half of ball with leaves, repeat same procedure on other half until leaves meet and entire tree top is covered. Tape on pears at random.

### 2. Partridge

*Body:* Cut body (A) of bird from sheet of mottled paper. Partridge colors are grays, browns and blues. Paper should be sturdy enough to hold shape, or lighter paper can be glued to cardboard cutout.

*Beak, shock, eye:* For beak, cut small triangle of gold paper and glue to body. For shock (head feather), cut bright-colored shape like elongated question mark. Use third color for eye, cut dot the size of small button, with smaller gold dot glued in center.

*Wing:* Wing (B) and feathers (C) may repeat four colors already used in body, beak, shock and eye. Cut basic wing shape and glue shoulder to body. Cut individual feathers in four sizes (about 6 of each) from pattern and glue on wing in bands of colors. Bands overlap; feathers toward wing tip are longest. Shortest feathers at shoulder go on last.

*Tail:* Cut elongated teardrops (D), in same four colors of bird, each color a different length. Apply to body as above—in overlapping bands. Tape completed partridge to tree.

### 3. Two Turtledoves

Turtledoves are far more exotic than ordinary doves, having orange plumage. Cut orange body (A), add slender triangles of another color for beaks. Eyes are black dots painted near beaks. Since both sides are visible, each dove needs two wings (B). Cut 4 basic wing shapes from third color, glue on orange shoulder patches (C). Four tail feathers (D) should repeat wing colors. Glue wings and tail feathers to turtledoves.

### 4. Three French Hens

Bodies (A) are mottled, wings (B), beaks and teardrop tail feathers (C) are orange. Assemble on stands as shown in diagram.

*Stand:* Cut strip of orange paper ½" wide x 3½" long, fold into 4 equal lengths. Unfold, form triangle by pasting fourth length to first length, thus giving double thickness to base of triangle. Cut slit across triangle and fit hen into slit.

### 5. Four Colly Birds

A colly bird (sometimes sung as "calling bird") is a blackbird. Bodies (A) are black, beaks orange. Orange wings (B) have gold shoulder patches (C). Tail feathers (D) are black. Assemble and tape colly birds to tree top.

### 6. Five Gold Rings.

Glue two pieces of gold paper back to back to make double thickness.

*partridge*

*one square equals 1"*

*cut out shock & attach*

*glue wing to body*

*two turtledoves*

*each square equals ½"*

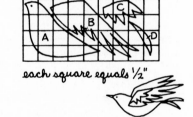

*three french hens*

*stand*

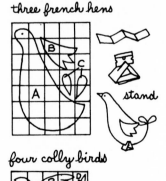

*four colly birds*

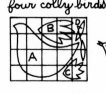

*five gold rings*

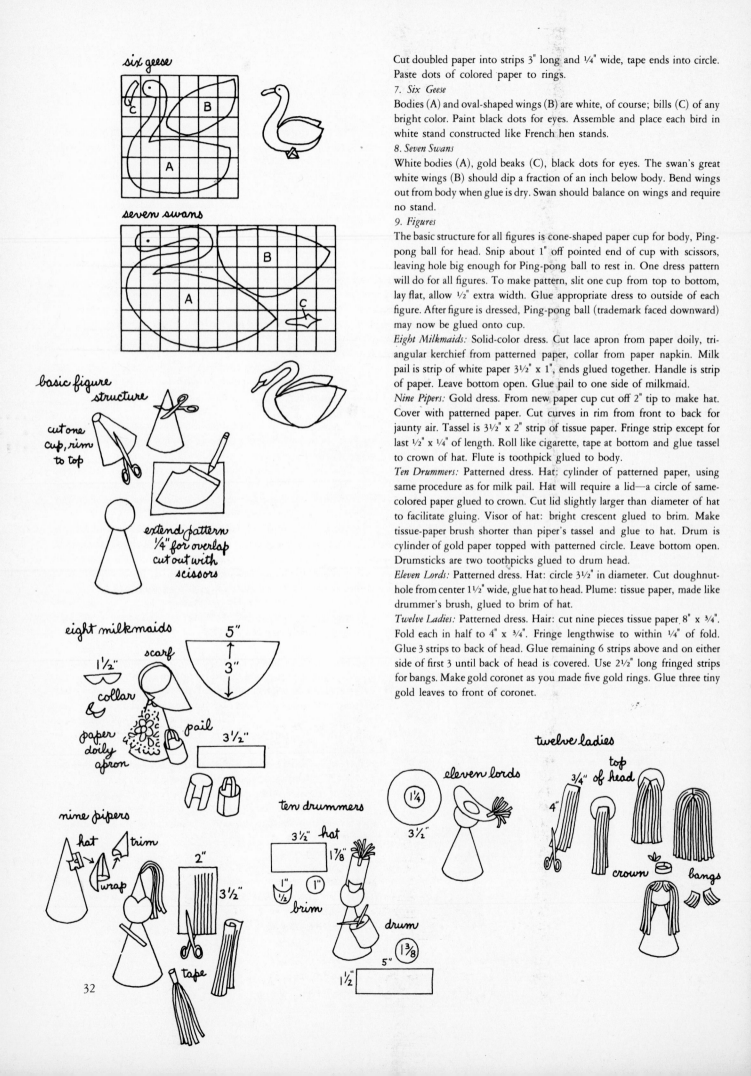

Cut doubled paper into strips 3" long and ¼" wide, tape ends into circle. Paste dots of colored paper to rings.

*7. Six Geese*
Bodies (A) and oval-shaped wings (B) are white, of course; bills (C) of any bright color. Paint black dots for eyes. Assemble and place each bird in white stand constructed like French hen stands.

*8. Seven Swans*
White bodies (A), gold beaks (C), black dots for eyes. The swan's great white wings (B) should dip a fraction of an inch below body. Bend wings out from body when glue is dry. Swan should balance on wings and require no stand.

*9. Figures*
The basic structure for all figures is cone-shaped paper cup for body, Ping-pong ball for head. Snip about 1" off pointed end of cup with scissors, leaving hole big enough for Ping-pong ball to rest in. One dress pattern will do for all figures. To make pattern, slit one cup from top to bottom, lay flat, allow ½" extra width. Glue appropriate dress to outside of each figure. After figure is dressed, Ping-pong ball (trademark faced downward) may now be glued onto cup.

*Eight Milkmaids:* Solid-color dress. Cut lace apron from paper doily, triangular kerchief from patterned paper, collar from paper napkin. Milk pail is strip of white paper 3½" x 1", ends glued together. Handle is strip of paper. Leave bottom open. Glue pail to one side of milkmaid.

*Nine Pipers:* Gold dress. From new paper cup cut off 2" tip to make hat. Cover with patterned paper. Cut curves in rim from front to back for jaunty air. Tassel is 3½" x 2" strip of tissue paper. Fringe strip except for last ½" x ¼" of length. Roll like cigarette, tape at bottom and glue tassel to crown of hat. Flute is toothpick glued to body.

*Ten Drummers:* Patterned dress. Hat: cylinder of patterned paper, using same procedure as for milk pail. Hat will require a lid—a circle of same-colored paper glued to crown. Cut lid slightly larger than diameter of hat to facilitate gluing. Visor of hat: bright crescent glued to brim. Make tissue-paper brush shorter than piper's tassel and glue to hat. Drum is cylinder of gold paper topped with patterned circle. Leave bottom open. Drumsticks are two toothpicks glued to drum head.

*Eleven Lords:* Patterned dress. Hat: circle 3½" in diameter. Cut doughnut-hole from center 1½" wide, glue hat to head. Plume: tissue paper, made like drummer's brush, glued to brim of hat.

*Twelve Ladies:* Patterned dress. Hair: cut nine pieces tissue paper 8" x ¾". Fold each in half to 4" x ¾". Fringe lengthwise to within ¼" of fold. Glue 3 strips to back of head. Glue remaining 6 strips above and on either side of first 3 until back of head is covered. Use 2½" long fringed strips for bangs. Make gold coronet as you made five gold rings. Glue three tiny gold leaves to front of coronet.

# EVERGREENS

## DELLA ROBBIA WREATH

*Photograph on page 22*

*Mossed wreath frame
(obtainable from florist)
Sprays of blue spruce 4" to 6"
long (prune from tree
or buy from florist)
Oranges, tangerines, lemons,
apples, grapes, kumquats,
Lady apples, walnuts,
acorns, rosettes of hen-and-
chickens (succulent rock plant)
Wire
Plastic (from dry cleaner)
(If wreath is large, all
fresh fruits will make it
heavy; mix with plastic fruits)*

Make rough cutout of wreath in plastic and bind it to back of wreath frame with string. String will be covered in front and plastic will prevent stain on door or wall. Twist ends of wire loop around frame for hanging wreath. Insert stems of spruce sprays into frame, piercing 2" into moss. Sprays should be inserted all around the outer and inner circumference. Cover the area between the two circumferences with more spruce. Do not stab in; lay flat and hold in place with bent wire or heavy hairpins. Wire the stem of each cluster of grapes and pierce wire into moss. Space clusters of grapes evenly around wreath. Pierce strong wire through bottoms of oranges, tangerines, lemons, apples and hen-and-chickens and insert two ends of wire into moss. Fill in between with kumquats, Lady apples, clusters of walnuts and acorns. If nuts are plastic, they will come in clusters. If real, twist thin wire around walnut's ridge (where it opens) and stem of acorn.

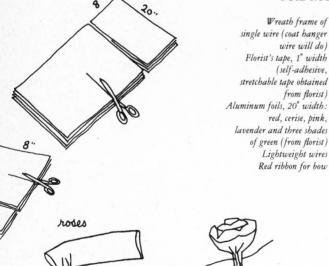

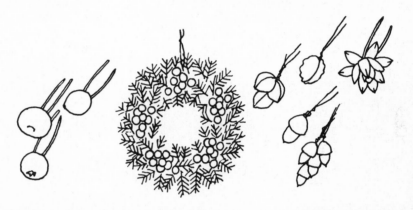

## FOIL ROSE WREATH

*Photograph on page 23*

*Wreath frame of
single wire (coat hanger
wire will do)
Florist's tape, 1" width
(self-adhesive,
stretchable tape obtained
from florist)
Aluminum foils, 20" width:
red, cerise, pink,
lavender and three shades
of green (from florist)
Lightweight wires
Red ribbon for bow*

Unroll all foil on floor, placing one color on top of another, greens on top. Measure length of foil in 8" segments and cut. Each segment is now 20" x 8". Remove three shades of green and cut each piece into thirds, each measuring 6⅔" x 8". Reserve for leaves.

*Roses:* Take each 20" x 8" piece of foil and fold in half. *Do not crease.* It now measures 20" x 4". Gather cut edges in series of tucks until foil forms a circle. Outer circumference will crinkle into petal effect. Pierce gathered tucks with wire. Twist wire to make stem and bind it with florist's tape.

*Leaves:* Take each 6⅔" x 8" piece of green foil and place before you so that 8" sides are horizontal, 6⅔" sides vertical. Fold into thirds. Right and left thirds will overlap, and resulting rectangle is one third of original size. Fold the left and right top corners in to bring rectangle to leaf point. Gather bottom into a stem and bind it tightly with wire. Cover wire with tape. Crease leaf down center.

Twist roses by their wires onto frame, adding leaves as you go. Put dark-green leaves on outer circumference to give wreath a defined border. Put leaves of two lighter shades between roses. Cover twisted wires on wreath frame with tape. Add wire loop for hanging wreath. Wire on bow; if wreath is used outside, make bow of water-repellent ribbon.

roses

leaves

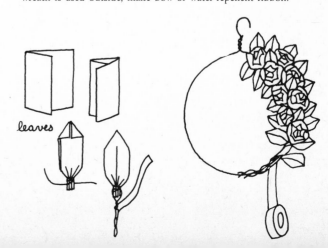

## FESTOON

*Photograph on page 25*

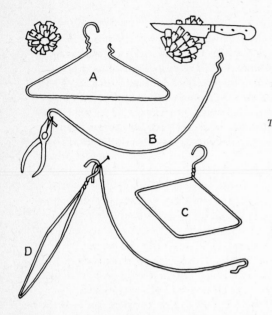

*Large and small pine cones*
*Brown pods, such as eucalyptus, jacaranda and sweet gum (obtainable from florist)*
*Fresh or plastic holly*
*Three yards of red ribbon, 3" wide*
*Three wire coat hangers*
*Pliers*
*Wires and florist's tape*

Slice large cones into rosettes. Wind wire around each rosette at bottom; twist ends of wire together, creating stem and tape stem. Wire and tape pods and holly stems. For the top of festoon, unwind a wire coat hanger (A) and bend length of hanger into crescent curve (B). Bend small hook-shape at either end. Bind cones, pods and holly to hanger by means of taped stems; place the greatest mass in center. The side pieces of the festoon are each one coat hanger. Grasp each hanger at hook and in middle of horizontal bar and pull (C). Hanger will stretch into a double wire with hook at one end. Bind on cones, pods, and holly. Cut ribbon in half, make each half into double bow with streamers. Hang center crescent by hooking ends on nails. Hook side pieces to same nails (D). Attach bows at corners to hide hooks.

## PYRAMID

*Photograph on page 25*

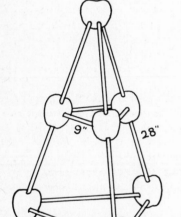

*¼" wooden doweling painted green: three 28" lengths, three 16" lengths, three 9" lengths*
*Seven large apples*
*Sprigs of evergreen about 6" long*
*Florist's wire, green twine*
*Cherries, Lady apples, yellow pears, small red apples*

Apples are used to hold together this pyramid of dowels decorated with fruits and greenery. Whittle 1" points on ends of all dowels. Drive each of the 28" dowels through a large apple and slide apple to midpoint. Now impale a large apple onto one end of each of the 28" dowels. Stab apples in cheek rather than through core, so as apples sit, dowels are at angle. Wire stems of cherries, pierce wire through bottoms of larger fruits and twist ends together. Bind evergreen sprigs to 16" and 9" dowels with green twine, covering dowels completely. Connect three end apples with 16" dowels, forming base of pyramid. Connect apples at midpoint with 9" dowels. Stick other ends of three long dowels into single apple to form apex. Bind sprigs and wire fruits beneath apple at apex. Wire fruits to 9" dowels. Set pyramid on cloth or tray. Nestle or wire remaining fruits among evergreens of base. Pyramid will look fresh for several days, but a small amount of fruit juices may drip onto cloth.

## ESPALIER TREE

*Photograph on page 25*

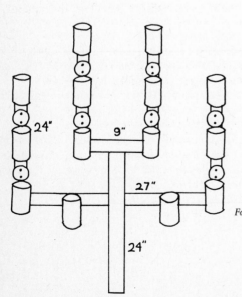

*Clear pine lengths 1¼" x 2":*
*4 pieces 24" long,*
*1 piece 9" long, one piece 27" long*
*1 piece framing fir, 2" x 3" x 24"*
*Hammer, nails*
*14 cans 3" high, open lids still attached*
*42 large red glass balls*
*126 small red glass balls*
*70 large English ivy leaves*
*Holly, ivy, gold spray*
*Large pot for base,*
*4" thick styrofoam to fit in pot*
*Florist's moss, wire*
*Fourteen 4" squares chicken wire*

Build the wooden frame with hammer and nails. Nail the 14 tin cans to the frame, 3 cans on each upright, 2 on the lower horizontal. To nail can, drive 2 nails in lid. Fill each can with crumpled chicken wire, in which you will insert plants. Spray entire tree, frame and cans with gold spray, following instructions on spray can. Fit pot with styrofoam, sand or soil. Wedge trunk of tree in styrofoam, sand or soil. Cover top of styrofoam with florist's moss or green paper. If you like, paint the edge of ivy leaves with gold paint (spray gold into glass, dip brush in glass). Make a bouquet (one for each of 14 cans) of 3 large and 9 small balls and 5 ivy leaves, the bouquet held at the stems with wire. Fill cans with water, insert bouquets. Add fresh holly and ivy.

# THE CHRISTMAS PACKAGE

*Photograph on page 26*

*Cellophane tape*
*Casein glue, rubber cement*
*Hole puncher, scissors*
*Single-edged razor blade*
*Wrappings, ribbons and bows*
*Gold trim*
*Bookmark*
*Sealing wax, pen and ink*
*Print tea towel*

Unless otherwise specified, all packages are wrapped in standard manner. Always tape lid of box to box itself on all sides to hold lid in and make neater wrap. Tape is used where bond is visually unimportant, casein glue is used where bond is visually important, provided materials will not be wrinkled or stained by glue. Rubber cement is used where bond is visually important and where glue would wrinkle or stain materials or where object cemented must be removable. Innumerable variations in color, size, shape, placement of decorations, etc., can be made on directions below.

(A) Use striped wrapping paper and paste lengths of matching ribbon crosswise to paper stripes to form plaid.

(B) Cut plain paper to exact size for wrapping. Place box in center of paper and trace outline of bottom on reverse of paper. Draw tree within the rectangle and cut out with razor blade. Paste green paper on reverse of wrapping paper over the body of the tree. Paste brown paper over trunk. Wrap package, making sure tree is in center of front. Decorate the tree by punching dots from colored papers and using a dab of cement to glue these on as "ornaments."

(C) A name card can be made from a rectangular scrap of wrapping paper. Fold in half with back of paper inside. Write name or message inside. Decorate half of outside with gold trim, glue other half to package.

(D) Contents of package may be suggested by wrapping. For example, wrap book like standard package, then paste bookmark to front, using rubber cement. For tie, attach tie clip to seam. For scarf, fasten pin or costume clip to box.

(E) Cut a jagged edge on one side of a colorful piece of scrap paper. Cement along upper edge of package. Cut crescent for eyes, a triangle nose and a long crescent mouth. Make tie from a ribbon ring. Tie different color ribbon around center of ring for knot and cement to package.

(F) Make one large sheet of wrapping paper by taping together two sheets of contrasting colors. Tape on reverse side of paper. When wrapping package, place seam of papers off-center. Place bow so one half is on each kind of paper.

(G) To make name-window, wrap box in dark paper. Take two short lengths of light-colored ribbon and notch one end of each. Using gold-wrapped chocolate "coin" or other gold ornament, make medallion by pasting ribbons to package in inverted V and gluing medallion over ribbons. Cut rectangle in paper, off-center. Slide contrasting strip of paper through window and glue to lid of box for name plate.

(H) Punch double row of holes along one edge of paper. Tape narrow ribbon to back of paper under one row, tape second ribbon of contrasting color to back of second row.

(I) Wrap package in print fabric instead of paper. A tea towel will do.

(J) Cut one upper-case and one lower-case letter (perhaps your child's initial). Glue them on opposite sides of box, paste bells, stars, trees, etc., to other four sides. Frame each face of cube with hand-drawn line or colorful tape.

(K) Cement gold trim around edge of package to form a frame.

(L) To brighten gift certificate, remove certificate from envelope and steam envelope open at all seams. Using it as a pattern, trace opened envelope on reverse of wrapping paper, then cut out, fold and glue to form a new envelope. For stamp, cut rectangle of contrasting paper and punch half-holes around edges. Draw simulated postmark. "Cancel" stamp by drawing a series of wavy lines over stamp and postmark.

## RECESSED PICTURE LID

*Photograph on page 26*

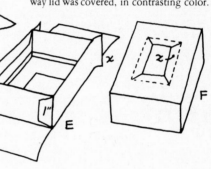

*Box, larger than picture to be framed, with lid nearly as deep as box*
*Cellophane tape*
*Casein glue or library paste*
*Fabric or paper for covering*
*Cellophane*
*Pencil*
*Ruler*
*Single-edged razor blade*
*Scissors*
*Light cardboard*

Remove lid. From top edge of box, cut ¼"-deep piece from around box, forming frame (A). Glue frame inside lid (B). Trace rectangle the size of picture on top of lid and cut out (C). Cover lid: Fabric or paper must be big enough to cover top and all sides of lid, plus 1" extra on all sides. Stand lid on its long side 1" back from long edge of covering, equidistant from ends (D). Snip 1" into covering at points *v*, fold flap *w* inside lid and glue (use library paste for fabric, casein glue for paper). Turn lid on other long edge keeping covering taut across top. Cut second 1" flap and glue to inside of lid. To cover remaining ends (E), cut away excess material *x*. Fold 1" flaps *y* to lid ends and glue. Fold bigger end flaps and glue. Cut rectangle in covering with dimensions ½" smaller on every side than window in lid (F). Snip a diagonal at each corner, fold down flaps *z* and glue. Cut piece of light cardboard to inside dimensions of lid. Place inside lid until cardboard rests on ¼" frame previously glued inside lid. Trace rectangle the size of window on cardboard and remove. Glue picture in center of traced rectangle. Frame inside of window with narrow decorative trim glued to underside. Tape cellophane on inside of lid to cover window opening (taping over back of trim), then set cardboard with glued-on picture on frame inside lid and tape into place. Cover bottom of box in same way lid was covered, in contrasting color. Completed parcel shown in (G).

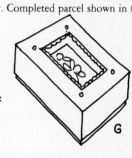

## TREASURE CHEST

*Photograph on page 26*

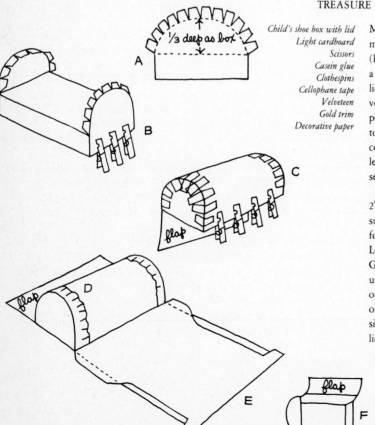

*Child's shoe box with lid*
*Light cardboard*
*Scissors*
*Casein glue*
*Clothespins*
*Cellophane tape*
*Velveteen*
*Gold trim*
*Decorative paper*

Measure short end of lid. Cut two pieces from light cardboard to this measurement, as illustrated (A), and glue to lid, using clothespins as clamps (B). Cut piece of light cardboard of a width equal to length of lid and of a length to cover curved lid and reach to bottom of entire box. Glue to lid and tape to curved side pieces (C). Cut 2 rectangular pieces of velveteen, each 1" wider than short side of lid and longer by 3" than highest point of lid. These will cover semicircular ends of lid. Glue width of one to inside width of lid, covering inside lid-band completely. Clip cloth at corners, pull taut over outside of semicircle. Trim excess around curve, leaving ½" for gluing. Trim and glue at corners as necessary, glue to semicircle and ½" over top (D). Repeat at other end.

Velveteen to cover outside of lid is 1" wider than long side of lid and 2" longer than distance around curved lid to bottom of flap (E). Glue sufficient amount on inside of front of lid-band to cover. Clip at corners, fold over ¼" on each side of material by turning in and gluing down. Leave one inch unfolded at end of material. Pull velveteen taut over lid. Glue along edges of curved lid and onto flap, turn remaining material under flap and glue. Cut second piece of material which will cover inside of lid, plus 1". Glue to inside of lid and 1" down flap (F). Now cut piece of velveteen for hinge band to length of box and 2" wide. Glue ½" to inside back edge of box, pull taut, glue remainder to back of box. Take lid and glue flap to this side of box, gluing over hinge band. *Glue as*

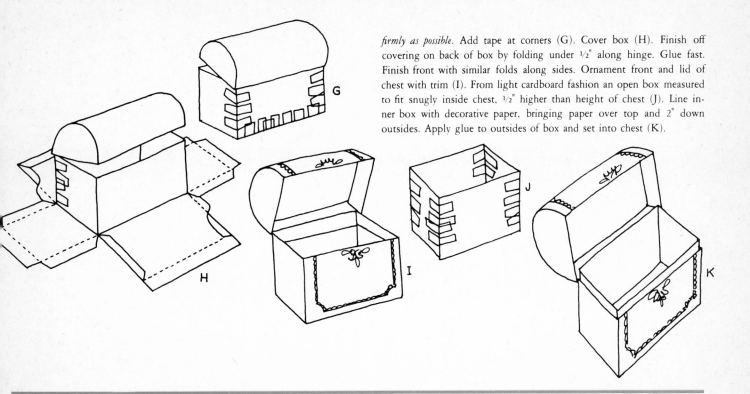

*firmly as possible.* Add tape at corners (G). Cover box (H). Finish off covering on back of box by folding under ½" along hinge. Glue fast. Finish front with similar folds along sides. Ornament front and lid of chest with trim (I). From light cardboard fashion an open box measured to fit snugly inside chest, ½" higher than height of chest (J). Line inner box with decorative paper, bringing paper over top and 2" down outsides. Apply glue to outsides of box and set into chest (K).

## PINATA

*Photograph on page 27*

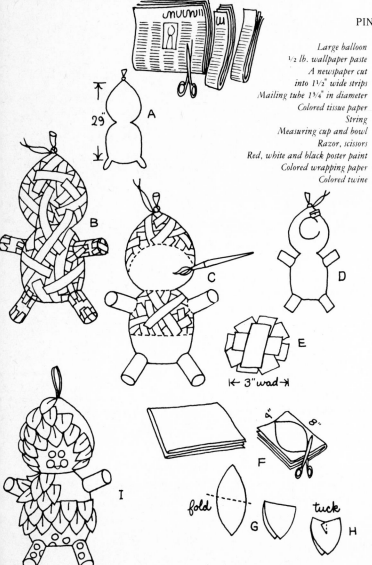

*Large balloon*
*½ lb. wallpaper paste*
*A newspaper cut*
*into 1½" wide strips*
*Mailing tube 1¾" in diameter*
*Colored tissue paper*
*String*
*Measuring cup and bowl*
*Razor, scissors*
*Red, white and black poster paint*
*Colored wrapping paper*
*Colored twine*

Inflate an animal balloon (any balloon with neck) so that body and head, but not ears, are distended. If balloon with neck is unavailable, form one by belting an oval balloon with tape. Balloon should measure 29" from base of ears to stem (A). Knot stem and tie with 6" length of string. Prepare 3 cups paste by instructions on bag. Dip newspaper strips in paste and smooth over balloon. Criss-cross strips, rubbing smooth after each application. Cut four lengths of mailing tube each 4" long. Place two lengths for legs, two for arms, and secure to body with newspaper strips ½" wide. Criss-cross entire balloon with strips until no balloon color can be seen (B). Be sure to cover open ends of mailing tubes and build up with many layers of strips around knot. Leave knot uncovered. Hang balloon from string to dry for 24 hours. Paint face and arms of piñata pink (mix white and a little red poster paint), trousers and legs black (C). When dry, puncture balloon near knot. Balloon will collapse gently. Cut flap 5" in diameter in back of head (D), leaving 2" of circumference attached as a hinge. Remove collapsed balloon through flap. Seal hole where balloon stem was from inside with 3" x 3" wad of paste-moistened newspaper strips (E), reaching through flap. In 24 hours when wad is dry, jab small hole in center with knitting needle. Tie both ends of 12" length of pink twine into knot. Loop twine and thread loop through hole in wad, again reaching through flap. Knot will stop loop from pulling through. Cut petals from various shades of red tissue paper (F). Eight or 16 petals can be cut at one time by folding paper 3 or 4 times. Petals should be 8" long from tip to tip, 3" across at widest point. Fold petal in half on a slightly diagonal line so that points don't line up (G). To make petal puffy, take ½" tuck along diagonal fold (H). Apply paste to fold and attach petal to body. Above trousers apply petals in overlapping rows, starting at bottom and working up. Do same around head, covering entire body except face, trousers and ends of arms (I). Close opening in back and paste petals on it, concealing but not sealing it up. Cut two circles out of black paper and apply as eyes. Apply two circles of pink paper as rosy cheeks. A small half circle of red paper serves as mouth. From shiny black paper cut out circles and paste on trousers. Fill cavity with candies.

# FOR CHRISTMAS

*The poem below, describing the hurry and excitement of the city streets at Christmastime, was written by the American novelist Rachel Field ( 1894-1942). Best-selling author of "All This, and Heaven Too," Miss Field wrote poems and books for children, as well as adult novels.*

Now not a window small or big
But wears a wreath or holly sprig;
Nor any shop too poor to show
Its spray of pine or mistletoe.
Now city airs are spicy-sweet
With Christmas trees along each street,
Green spruce and fir whose boughs will hold
Their tinseled balls and fruits of gold.
Now postmen pass in threes and fours
Like bent, blue-coated Santa Claus.
Now people hurry to and fro
With little girls and boys in tow,
And not a child but keeps some trace
Of Christmas secrets in his face.

# TINSELED WITH FROST

The timeless meaning of the Christmas tree, hung with lights on Christmas Eve, is evoked in the poem below, entitled *"The Christmas Tree,"* by the contemporary English poet, critic and novelist, C. Day Lewis.

*Put out the lights now!*
*Look at the Tree, the rough tree dazzled*
*In oriole plumes of flame,*
*Tinselled with twinkling frost fire, tasselled*
*With stars and moons—the same*

*That yesterday hid in the spinney and had no fame*
*Till we put out the lights now.*

*Hard are the nights now:*
*The fields at moonrise turn to agate,*
*Shadows are cold as jet;*
*In dyke and furrow, in copse and faggot*
*The frost's tooth is set;*
*And stars are the sparks whirled out by the north wind's*
*    fret*
*On the flinty nights now.*

*So feast your eyes now*
*On mimic star and moon-cold bauble:*
*World may wither unseen,*
*But the Christmas tree is a tree of fable—*
*A phoenix in evergreen,*
*And the world cannot change or chill what its mysteries*
*    mean*
*To your hearts and eyes now.*

*The vision dies now*
*Candle by candle: the tree that embraced it*
*Returns to its own kind,*
*To be earthed again and weather as best it*
*May the frost and the wind.*
*Children, it too had its hour—you will not mind*
*If it lives or dies now.*

# One Way Out of the Gift~Giving Dilemma

*The selection of presents for a long list of friends is one of the worries of Christmas. In this extract from "A Hint for Next Christmas," British writer A. A. Milne ( 1882-1956) solves the problem as it arose at a Christmas house party.*

And now I am reminded of the ingenuity of a friend of mine, William by name, who arrived at a large country house for Christmas without any present in his bag. He had expected neither to give nor to receive anything, but to his horror he discovered on the 24th that everybody was preparing a Christmas present for him, and that it was taken for granted that he would require a little privacy and brown paper on Christmas Eve for the purpose of addressing his own offerings to others. He had wild thoughts of telegraphing to London for something to be sent down, and spoke to other members of the house-party in order to discover what sort of presents would be suitable.

"What are you giving our host?" he asked . . .

"Mary and I are giving him a book," said John, referring to his wife.

William then approached the youngest son of the house, and discovered that he and his next brother Dick were sharing in this, that, and the other. When he had heard this, William retired to his room and thought profoundly.

He was the first down to breakfast on Christmas morning. All the places at the table were piled high with presents. He looked at John's place. The top parcel said, "To John and Mary from Charles." William took out his fountain-pen and added a couple of words to the inscription. It then read, "To John and Mary from Charles and William," and in William's opinion looked just as effective as before. He moved on to the next place. "To Angela from Father," said the top parcel. "And William," wrote William. At his hostess' place he hesitated for a moment. The first present there was for "Darling Mother, from her loving children." It did not seem that an "and William" was quite suitable. But his hostess was not to be deprived of William's kindly thought; twenty seconds later the handkerchiefs "from John and Mary and William" expressed all the nice things which he was feeling for her. He passed on to the next place. . . .

It is of course impossible to thank every donor of a joint gift; one simply thanks the first person whose eye one happens to catch. Sometimes William's eye was caught, sometimes not. But he was spared all embarrassment; and I can recommend his solution of the problem with perfect confidence to those who may be in a similar predicament . . .

# Deck the Halls

*This old Welsh carol is in the style of the English madrigals which were very popular in the late 16th Century and which followed each line of verse with a repeating refrain. Children love its gaiety and its simple rhythm.*

Deck the halls with boughs of hol-ly!
'Tis the sea-son to be jol-ly!
Fa la la la la la la la la.

Don we now our gay ap-pa-rel, Fa la la la la la la la la.

Troll the an-cient Yule-tide ca-rol, Fa la la la la la la la la.

# II
# HOLIDAY HOSPITALITY

THE CHRISTMAS TABLE WAS SO long and there were so many of us, that a few of the chairs were caught in a jog of the wall and had no proper approach except by crawling on hands and knees beneath it. Each year it was customary to request my maiden aunt, a prim lady who bordered on seventy and had limbs instead of legs, to undertake the passage. Each year we listened for the jest and shouted with joy when the request was made.... Then another cousin, who journeyed sometimes to New York, usually instructed us in the latest manner of eating an orange in the metropolis. But we disregarded his fashionable instruction, and peeled ours round and round. The dinner itself was a prodigious feast. The cookstove must have rested and panted for a week thereafter. Before long, Annie got so red bringing in turkeys and cranberry sauce —countless plates heaped and toppling with vegetables and meats—that one might think she herself was in process to become a pickled beet and would presently enter on a platter.

"CHIMNEY-POT PAPERS," CHARLES S. BROOKS

A HAPPY FAMILY *and a hungry cat in this illustration can hardly wait to begin the merry Christmas feast. Even the fish smiles.*

# DELIGHTS
# OF THE
# HOLIDAY
# TABLE

THROUGHOUT THE WORLD, *families gather for Christmas dinner. A simple grace: "For Food and Fellowship, thank God."*

"BE NOT FORGETFUL to entertain strangers," St. Paul admonished the Hebrews, "for thereby some have entertained angels unawares."

A charming Bible story tells how Abraham welcomed to his tent three celestial visitors. Without knowing who the strangers were or why they had come, he hastened to bring them cool water, cakes of fine meal, and lamb with milk and butter sauce. "And he stood by them under the tree, and they did eat."

From the earliest times, man has offered food and drink as an expression of good will. The bread shared with his guest by the poorest peasant meant "welcome" no less than the lavish banquets held in the courts of kings. So it is that the great feast of Christmas has come to symbolize man's willingness to open his house and heart to the stranger as well as to the friend.

In Elizabethan England, following a long tradition of merrymaking at Christmastime, a nobleman often entertained guests in his halls from Christmas Eve until the Epiphany. Every night there were festive sup-

pers attended by servants bearing wax torches and trumpeters playing merry music; after dinner the Master of the Revels sang a song or carol, and all the company joined in the singing and dancing.

At the Christmas feast itself, a boar's head was served in the ceremonious manner established as early as Anglo-Saxon times. Garlanded with rosemary, its mouth propped open by an apple or a lemon, and laid upon a silver platter, the boar's head was borne in procession to the high table, while the entire company sang a favorite carol.

Since the boar's head had very little meat upon it, it was served to satisfy custom rather than the appetites of hungry guests. There were also great pies, steaming hot and filled with geese and turkeys, game and small birds, mutton and pork. There were ale and wine in great quantity, and finally the mince pie or plum soup which was later to evolve into plum pudding.

Not even the disapproval of the Puritans could quell the popular fondness for feasting at Christmas —when plum puddings were forbidden, it is said that many people sent to the Continent for them.

A mammoth community plum pudding was traditionally served every 50 years in the village of Paignton, in Devon, but so great were the difficulties of preparing it that the custom was eventually abandoned. The recipe for the great pudding of 1819 included four hundredweights of flour, 120 pounds of suet, an equal amount of raisins and a large number of eggs. After three days' boiling, the 900-pound delicacy was drawn by three horses to Paignton Green, where disappointed villagers discovered that it was not done in the middle.

Americans of this period tended to celebrate Christmas in the tradition of the countries from which they came. Thus, Southern planters followed the English custom of full houses and full larders. Cookies, cakes and pies were baked weeks in advance, turkeys were fattened and hams cured, jellies and jams were brought up from the cellar in preparation for the visiting friends and relatives who came in wagons and carriages from miles away and might stay on for weeks.

Today there is no longer need for such an astonishing quantity of food as was placed on the great Elizabethan tables, or even on the Christmas boards of our American ancestors. The modern Christmas dinner is usually a more intimate gathering of family. But the tradition of hospitality remains. The scattered members of a family may cross the continent by plane in order to be home for Christmas, lonely aunts or cousins are recalled to the family circle, and the stranger in town is remembered at this season of the year and invited to share the turkey and dressing.

At Christmas the house must be open as at no other time of the year. Children on holiday from school bring friends into the kitchen to pop corn or pull taffy; frost-nipped carolers must be cheered with hot chocolate, casual acquaintances who drop in with greetings are offered coffee and cake. Then there are buffet dinners, punch parties, late suppers after midnight church services. And, of course, there is the annual Christmas basket, filled with ham or turkey, vegetables, fruits and nuts, to be delivered to the home of some poor family. Giving, in the form of food and welcome, is one of the most basic pleasures of Christmas.

AT CHRISTMASTIME *there are parties, parties, parties. Some may be grand, with lavish buffets and bowls of punch. Some may be casual gatherings for hot chocolate and sandwiches after skating or caroling. And sometimes it is a party just to visit Grandmother, who has Christmas cookies and candy and almost always (as above) a big bowl of mixed nuts to crack before the fire.*

TO RESTORE STAMINA *of exhausted guests, refreshments are passed at a late-18th Century Christmas party after a lively game of Musical Chairs.*

# THE TEMPTING SIDEBOARD

Whether at an 18th Century gathering where games were all the rage, or at 20th Century cocktails where the recreation is mostly conversational, things to eat served elsewhere than in the dining room have long been part of a party. Guests may have to juggle them and consume them standing up. They may be called hors d'oeuvres, canapé or appetizers. They may be a light prelude to a large dinner or honest nourishment for a long, dinnerless evening. But because they are for guests, and for a party, they must be delicious.

Those shown here are especially appropriate for Christmas because although none is an hors d'oeuvre in its country of origin, all are traditional holiday foods. In Italy, *bagna cauda,* meaning "hot bath," is a light family meal at which everyone dips such delicacies as endives, peppers and the stems of baby artichokes into a piquant sauce. English meat pies can be adapted to the hors d'oeuvre tray by being baked in miniature. Germans enjoy pickled herring at Christmastime, and the French come home from celebrating midnight Mass to break fast on Christmas morning with pâté or a bite of chilled oyster and hot sausage.

44

TIERED DELICACIES *on a silver epergne are: (top) tender celery hearts, crisp endive, peppers and other raw vegetables; (middle) spicy herring salad, and plump pork and veal pies; (bottom) oysters on crushed ice. The bowl contains a hot dip for the vegetables, the center platter has hot sausages to go with ice-cold oysters, and at right is a dish of pâté. (Recipes pages 64-65.)*

SWEDISH RICE PORRIDGE *contains one almond; the finder, legend says, will wed within a year. (Recipe page 65.)*

LAMB SOUP *is a traditional first course at Lebanese Christmas dinners. Shown with it are a loaf of round, flat bread, fresh goat's milk cheese and assorted fruits. (Recipe page 65.)*

TORTELLINI IN BRODO, *eaten with nearly every Christmas dinner in Italy, is pasta in broth. (Recipe page 66.)*

# AN INTERNATIONAL ARRAY OF TRADITIONAL SOUPS

Soup has been an important part of man's fare almost since he discovered fire. Many a meal has come entire out of the soup kettle. Hungry Esau sold his birthright for a mess of pottage (probably a thick soup) presumably because it would fill him up. In its more sophisticated usage as a first course, soup is a clear broth that whets the appetite for the meal to come. But thick or clear, plain or fancy, the preparation of soup calls for patience and artistry. It has been said that the woman who cannot cook a good one should not be permitted to marry. Juices are unlocked from meats by slow simmering, and the variations of ingredients are countless. Meats, vegetables, fruits, nuts—anything edible can go into soup.

Because soup has been a staple for most of the world's peoples, legends and customs have flourished around it. The Norwegians believe that a bowl of rice porridge should be placed in the barn on Christmas Eve for the *Julenisser,* or Christmas gnomes. And the Lebanese, who traditionally kill a lamb on Christmas as a sacrifice to Christ, give most of the meat to the poor. The remainder is saved for their lamb soup.

POTAGE NOEL, *a creamy French onion soup served at Christmas, is much thicker than ordinary onion soup. Unashamedly rich, the soup can serve as a midday lunch or late supper, especially when accompanied by fresh French bread and a light rosé wine. (Recipe page 65.)*

47

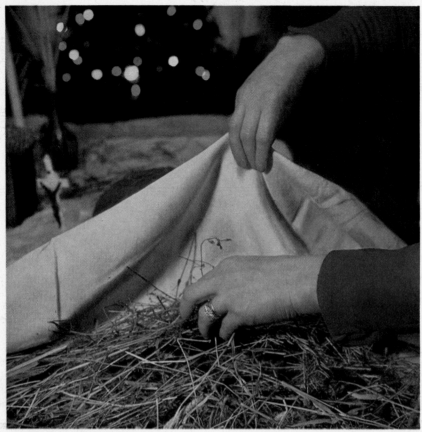

AN OLD TRADITION *is followed in a new land as a Polish-American mother spreads straw under the tablecloth at the Christmas Eve dinner to symbolize the manger. The meal is meatless.*

# A BOUNTIFUL LARDER FROM THE SEA

Amid the procession of masterpieces that follow one another to the table at Christmastime, fish, ancient symbol of Christianity, plays an important part. Many Christians around the world fast during Advent—a fast that traditionally reaches its climax with an excellent fish dinner on Christmas Eve. Afterward, midnight Mass is attended in the churches and cathedrals of Christendom, and the fast is at an end.

One of the best Christmas Eve recipes, the traditional *lutfisk,* comes from Scandinavia, where, since the Reformation, it has been customarily served preceding a rosy ham. *Lutfisk* is young, tender cod preserved in ashes, then by tradition sun-dried from December 9 until Christmas Eve. Another delicacy, widely enjoyed all over Europe, is stuffed carp. The grandeur of these great, long-lived fish—legends say Louis XIV hand-fed some that are still swimming in the ponds at Versailles—is recalled when they are basted with beer, wine, onion and gingersnaps.

A VARIED SELECTION *of dishes for Christmas includes fish. At bottom right is Swedish "lutfisk," or creamed cod. The shrimp casserole, to the left, is Spanish. The stuffed carp at center is a Polish dish, and at the top is a plate of Italian pasta with clams. (Recipes page 66.)*

# THE MONARCH OF THE CHRISTMAS TABLE

"Turkey," said the eminent French gastronome Brillat-Savarin, "is certainly one of the finest gifts made by the New World to the Old."

Though it originated in the Americas, the fowl that eased the early hardships of the pilgrims and that dominates Christmas and Thanksgiving tables is by no means solely an American dish. After its introduction into the Old World in the 16th Century, its size and flavor quickly made it a favorite for festive meals in many parts of Europe. Its European debut was probably made in Spain, when the conquistadors included a number of the leggy birds among the exotic novelties they brought back from Mexico to astonish the court. Today, turkey is essential to a Spanish Christmas. Housewives in Seville select their fowls from a flock driven through the town before Christmas, bargaining with the seller from open doors and windows.

In France, the popularity of the turkey dates back to the time of Louis XVI, when its vogue was part of the wave of enthusiasm for everything American that followed the colonial Revolution. The French still enjoy it, and cooked with chestnuts it is the mainstay of the Christmas menu in Burgundy. In England, turkey has replaced roast goose on most Christmas tables. As early as the 18th Century, the poet John Gay wrote of Christmas:

> From the low peasant to the lord
> The turkey smokes on every board.

# HOLIDAY
# DINNERS
# WITH
# A DIFFERENCE

Christmas dinner need not mean turkey. It may mean a crackling roast goose stuffed with apples and onions, a plump capon garnished with pignolias, or a savory baked ham. Each of these dishes is a Christmas favorite in some part of the world, and each has a long Christmas tradition

behind it. The goose was the Christmas meal of ordinary Englishmen, while the aristocracy feasted splendidly on swans and peacock pie. The advent of the turkey, however, made changes in people's eating habits. By the end of the 18th Century, turkeys were so well liked that 1,000 a day

OVEREATING AT CHRISTMAS *is satirized in this engraving by* **William Heath***. This voracious country family typifies a well-nourished England of the 1800s.*

OLDER FOOD TRADITIONS *are a stuffed capon (foreground), a roast goose (upper left) and a baked ham (right). All of these preceded the turkey as a holiday specialty. Capon is an Italian Christmas dish, while goose is widely eaten in Germany. "Merry Christmas" decorates the Swedish ham. (Recipes pages 67-68.)*

were being sent to London for Christmas from Norwich alone. In what must have been memorable processions, sometimes taking over a week, the birds made the journeys from farm to city on foot, shod in leather boots by their owners.

The capon was among the many game birds served at medieval and Elizabethan Christmas feasts. One of the old boar's head carols lists for the second course: cranes, herons, bitterns, partridges, plover, woodcock and snipe, "Larks in hot stew for the ladies to pick," and "Capons well baked, with knuckles of the roe, Raisins and currants, and other spices too."

The Scandinavian Christmas ham may stem from the Norse myth of the sacred boar, food of heroes in Valhalla. On Norwegian farms today, a special Christmas pig is fattened every year for the Yuletide table.

# THE MAKINGS
# FOR
# SAVORY
# STUFFINGS

Buttery oysters contrasted with crisp celery, the flavor of apple balanced against the flavor of onion, the pungency of red wine laced with the fleeting taste of herbs and spices—these hardly belong in the category of an afterthought to the Christmas turkey or goose. The well-seasoned stuffing supplies more than an extra taste; it is a noble counterpoint of flavors.

Man has always loved to dress up and flavor his foods. An important

stimulant to the age of exploration was spices—valued as highly as silks or gold or jewels. Small ships set sail for distant spice islands to please such tastes as that of the elegant lords and ladies of Spain for cinnamon in their cocoa.

English cooks were as extravagant flavorers of food as any. Such was their enthusiasm for saffron that some foods were served bright yellow. Their ardor for mixtures led to all sorts of fanciful creations. One

15th Century dish consisted of the fore part of a capon sewn to the after part of a suckling pig, the whole stuffed with eggs, breadcrumbs, saffron and mutton suet, and roasted on a spit. But perhaps the ultimate in flavoring comes from the French. A recipe of Napoleon's chancellor called for stuffing a turkey with a capon, the capon with a partridge, the partridge with a quail and the quail with an ortolan with an olive inside *it*. Only the olive was eaten.

WOODEN SPICE MILL AND APPLE PARER *(above) date from before the Civil War. Antique devices such as these helped American housewives prepare the stuffing for the Christmas goose.*

PART OF THE TREASURE HOUSE *of foods used to flavor other foods is displayed opposite. Americans have long used bread, onions, apples, chestnuts and oysters for stuffing. Readily available today are olive oil from Italy, wine and truffles from France, and cheeses and spices from around the world. Most meats, fish and poultry are improved with stuffing. (Recipes page 68.)*

55

# PUDDING, PIE AND A FRENCH CONFECTION

Spicy pies, fruity puddings and rich pastries have been the traditional Christmas-dinner desserts for hundreds of years. Plum pudding began as the "plum soup" of medieval England, combining mutton stock and fruits, including the prunes for which it was named. By the 16th Century the soup had been enriched into a pie including meat and suet which was cooked in a rectangular mold to represent Christ's manger. The Christmas pie appears in the rhyme about Little Jack Horner, and according to legend, eating pie each day of Christmas ensures good luck throughout the year.

Such food proved too rich for Puritan rulers, who thought it impious and outlawed it. But the people, not to be done out of their favorite dessert, disguised it by making it round and calling it by a different name—"Minc'd pie." By the 18th Century it was sometimes cooked without pastry, emerging as plum pudding.

The mock yule log was baked by enterprising Parisian bakers as a symbol of the actual wood. While yule logs are still burned at Christmas in some rural areas of France, city dwellers seem perfectly content to substitute edible ones of cake.

A FLAMING PUDDING, *topped with holly, is tiny compared to a plum pie baked for Henry VIII. His chef used two bushels of flour, 24 pounds of butter and eight kinds of meat. It was so big— nine feet long and 165 pounds—that it was wheeled to the table on a cart. (Recipe page 69.)*

CHRISTMAS SWEETS *are mince pie and a yule log of cake. The spices in the pie represent the Magi's gifts. The log is the urban substitute for burning a real yule log. (Recipes pages 69-70.)*

A DOOMED DESSERT *causes consternation among the guests at this 18th Century Christmas dinner. Plum pudding, in one form or another, has been a Christmas tradition for centuries.*

57

# SWEET BREADS FOR ANY HOUR

A basic symbol of hospitality, bread takes many delectable forms during the most hospitable of festivals. Christmas in kitchens around the world is ushered in to the fragrance of baking—of browning buns, rising loaves, and sweet breads of all varieties. While a Mexican baker is glazing the fruit-studded cakes known as the Crowns of the Three Kings, a housewife in Greece may be preparing the simple cake, impressed with a print of her hand, that she calls the Bread of Christ. And the American housewife, expecting holiday guests for coffee and cake, may draw upon recipes from all over the world. Six of these special Christmas breads are shown here. At left are two almond-sprinkled honey braids. On a board next to them is a Hungarian nut roll. The pedestal server displays the old-fashioned cinnamon buns the Austrian calls Schnecken. Beside them are two raisin-studded Italian panettoni, and at front center is a sugar-coated German Stollen. The crown-shaped cake at the right is a Polish babka. *(Recipes pages 70-71.)*

59

HORSE WITH RIDER *is a simulated German "Lebkuchen" cookie, cast from an 1833 mold and painted by a Hamburg museum to look as fresh as originals, which were used as ornaments.*

# MANY-HUED AND SHAPELY COOKIES

Cookies, which add such aroma and color, as well as delectable eating, to Christmas celebrations, have a history thousands of years old. Almost 2,000 years before Christ, a well-fed Egyptian wrote "Cakes were my daily bread." We know from scenes painted in the tomb of Ramses III that the cakes pharaohs ate were what we know as cookies. Since the Egyptians, and possibly before, every culture has had its cookies.

Many peoples have used cookies as sacrifices to their gods. In China, when one angry god demanded a human sacrifice and no one volunteered, gingerbread men were substituted to mollify the god.

Ancient Germans of means sacrificed live horses to the king of their gods, Wotan. Poorer folk, who had no horses, gave cookie horses instead. And in Scandinavia, Thor, the god of thunder, was offered honey cakes at the winter solstice in hopes that he would be pleased and grant the people an abundant harvest.

Today, although cookies are sacrificed only to our appetites, they are eaten everywhere, and their popularity shows no signs of abating.

NINE KINDS OF COOKIES, *each shape made with different recipe, come from seven European countries. A child's name can be iced on the gay Swedish spice cookies. (Recipes pages 72-73.)*

CANDLELIGHT TOAST *in a present-day London tavern is reminiscent of the robust Dickensian Christmas celebrations of a century ago. The custom of toast*

## A LEGACY
## OF CHEERING
## WINTER DRINKS

62

Steaming drinks to warm winter-chilled bones are a Christmas tradition as old as the holiday itself. There are countless national recipes, but each aims for the same effect—a heightening of the merriment and good will the season evokes.

Wassail, which is perhaps the best known of Christmas drinks, originated with the Anglo-Saxons. The

word derives from *wes hāl,* meaning "be in health." In 18th Century England, the well-to-do sat around large tables and passed from hand to hand the wassail bowl with its delicious aroma, floating nut meats and bits of toast, wishing one another good health. The poorer people would take mugs bedecked with ribbons and go "a-wassailing" from door to

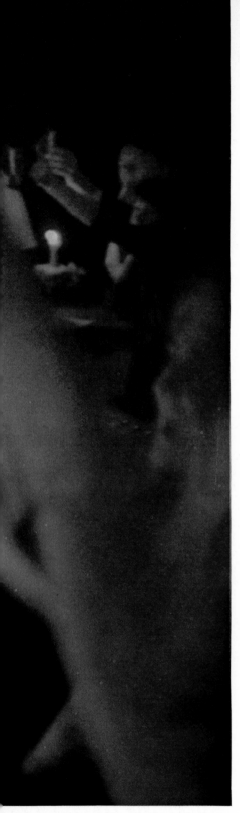

1,500 years old, was initiated by the Anglo-Saxons.

THREE NATIONAL DRINKS *to offer guests or chilly carolers are German "Selleriebowle" (left), English Christmas Carol Punch and frothy American Tom and Jerry. (Recipes page 73.)*

A BOWL OF GLOGG, *its spices, fruits and nuts adding to its heady aroma, is a Scandinavian Christmas recipe, served here in a 160-year-old wassail bowl from England. (Recipe page 73.)*

door, asking for money to buy a bit of the brew so they too could regale themselves.

Today the communal wassail bowl has long since been replaced by the clinking of glasses, and the toast no longer bobs merrily in the drink. But the tradition of toasting, so named because the liquor-soaked toast was considered a delicacy, still endures.

# APPETIZERS

## PATE MAISON

*Photograph on page 45*

*1 large onion, minced*
*2 tablespoons butter*
*½ cup cognac*
*¾ pound lean pork*
*½ pound veal*
*½ pound calves' liver or chicken livers*
*½ pound fresh pork fat*
*2 eggs*
*2 teaspoons salt*
*⅛ teaspoon pepper*
*⅛ teaspoon allspice*
*½ teaspoon thyme*
*1 clove garlic, minced*
*2 canned truffles, chopped*
*½ cup pistachio nuts, chopped*
*1 bay leaf*

Cook the onion in hot butter for 5 minutes, then turn into mixing bowl. Pour the cognac into the same pan and boil it down to ¼ cup. Meats and half the pork fat should be very finely ground together and it is best to have your butcher do this for you. Combine all ingredients except remaining pork fat and bay leaf and beat together until thoroughly blended and light. Pâtés should be seasoned perfectly when served. To determine whether or not flavor is just what you want, sauté a tablespoon of the mixture in a little butter and taste it. If necessary, mix in additional seasonings. Line the bottom and sides of a loaf pan with remaining pork fat very thinly sliced. Fill the pan with pâté mixture, lay bay leaf on top and cover with a piece of foil. Set in pan of hot water. Bake in a moderate oven (350°) for 1 hour and 40 minutes; the pâté should shrink from the sides of the pan and be surrounded with a clear yellow liquid (fat and juice). Remove pan from water and set out to cool. On top of the foil, place a weight so pâté will be solidly packed with no air holes—a 5-pound bag of sugar will just fit into a standard loaf pan and makes an excellent weight. Cool pâté for several hours, then chill overnight with weight on top. To serve pâté, unmold, garnish and slice. Surrounding layer of fat may be left on or removed, as desired. Serves 8-10.

## OYSTERS GASCOGNE

*Photograph on page 45*

*1½ dozen raw oysters*
*salt, pepper*
*2 lemons, quartered*
*1½ dozen tiny pork sausages*

Open oysters and leave in the deeper shell. If frozen or canned, use aluminum foil shells. Place on a bed of crushed ice with salt, freshly ground pepper and lemon quarters beside them. Prick sausages on each side, place in a skillet, add water to cover and bring to a boil. Drain, then cook over moderate heat for 10 minutes, or until brown and crisp. Eat seasoned chilled oyster followed by a hot sausage. Serves 8.

## PORK AND VEAL PIE

*Photograph on page 45*

*Pastry: 2 cups flour*
*¼ teaspoon salt*
*½ cup butter*
*3-4 tablespoons lard*
*1 egg, beaten*
*4-5 tablespoons cold milk*
*Filling: 1 pound lean pork, 1 pound veal*
*½ pound salt pork*
*1 large onion, minced*
*1 garlic clove, minced, ⅛ teaspoon ground cloves*
*3 tablespoons chopped parsley*
*1 tablespoon chopped celery leaves*
*¼ cup hot meat broth*
*Salt and pepper to taste*

Sift flour and salt into a bowl. Use a pastry blender or two knives to cut butter and lard into flour; mixture should resemble coarse corn meal. Add egg and milk to make a firm dough. Chill dough while preparing filling, but not longer than 1 hour. Have pork, veal and salt pork ground together. Turn meat mixture into a hot skillet over moderate heat. Add onion and garlic and cook mixture for about 5 minutes, or until it begins to brown, stirring constantly. Blend in remaining ingredients, cover, and reduce to low heat; cook 30 minutes, stirring several times. If mixture appears too dry, add boiling water a few tablespoons at a time. Roll out half the pastry and line a 10-inch pie pan; put filling in pie shell. Roll out remaining pastry, fold in half and make a few slits so steam can escape. Moisten edge of lower crust with water, lay top crust over filling with fold in center and unfold; press edges together and flute. Bake in a hot oven (425°) for 15 minutes; reduce heat to 375° and bake 25-30 minutes more, or until crust is a golden brown. Serve hot or cold as preferred; traditionally the pie is served chilled. Serves 8-10. *For hors d'oeuvre-sized pies:* Proceed as above, but use individual pastry tins to make pies. Recipe will make 24 little pies about 2 inches in diameter.

## BAGNA CAUDA

*Photograph on page 45*

1/4 cup butter, 1/4 cup olive oil
2 large garlic cloves, 8 anchovy fillets, mashed
1 canned white truffle, minced
1 cup heavy cream, scalded
4 carrots, cut in strips, 2 celery hearts, quartered
4 small endives, halved
1 green pepper, 1 red pepper, thinly slivered
Small bunch cardoons, cut in 4-inch sections

Simmer butter, olive oil and garlic together for 5-6 minutes; remove garlic. Add anchovies and truffle and blend until smooth. Stir in cream and simmer 2-3 minutes, or until very hot. Yields 1½ cups sauce. Arrange crisp vegetable buffet on platter, use sauce as hot dip. The young artichoke plant is known as a "cardoon." To prepare for eating, cut the stalks in pieces and place in a bowl of ice water with the juice of 2 lemons. Let stand 2-3 hours before using. Cardoons are a basic ingredient of *bagna cauda* in Italy, but dip may be used with any preferred vegetables.

## HERRING SALAD

*Photograph on page 45*

2 salt herring
2 cups diced cooked veal
1½ cups diced cooked beets
2 cups diced cooked potatoes
2 apples, peeled and diced
2 cucumber pickles, minced
6 tablespoons vinegar
2 tablespoons sugar
1/4 teaspoon pepper
1/2 teaspoon dry mustard
1/2 cup dairy sour cream

Clean the herring and soak overnight in cold water. Rinse thoroughly, drain, skin and bone. Cut off fillets and dice. Mix all the diced and minced ingredients in a large bowl. Combine vinegar with sugar and seasonings, pour over ingredients and mix well. Add sour cream. Pack salad tightly in a 2-quart mold and chill for 2 hours. To serve, turn out on cold platter. May be garnished with alternate white and yellow stripes of sieved hard-cooked egg. Serves 8.
*For appetizer servings:* Pack salad mixture tightly in individual molds; chill and serve as above. Makes 12 individual molds.

# SOUPS

## POTAGE NOEL

*Photograph on page 46*

5 tablespoons butter
4 tablespoons flour
2 quarts seasoned chicken broth
1/2 cup heavy cream
2 egg yolks
1 canned truffle, thinly sliced
3 tablespoons diced pimiento

Heat butter and stir in flour; simmer few minutes; add broth and continue simmering for about ½ hour, or until thick and smooth. Blend heavy cream with egg yolks, then add to soup, stirring constantly; simmer five minutes. Garnish with truffle slices and pimiento dice and serve. If available, whole raw cranberries may be used as garnish in place of pimiento. Serves 8-10.

## LEBANON LAMB SOUP

*Photograph on page 47*

1 pound boneless lamb, ground
1 tablespoon chopped parsley
1/2 teaspoon salt, 1/4 teaspoon pepper
2 tablespoons salad oil
1 tablespoon ground cinnamon
1/2 cup short-grain rice
2 cups tomato juice, 1/4 cup tomato purée

Mix lamb, parsley and seasonings; shape into small balls. Brown lamb balls in hot oil, then reduce heat to moderate and continue cooking for 10 minutes. Heat 2 quarts water in a large kettle, add cinnamon and lamb balls; simmer over low heat for 20 minutes. Stir in rice, tomato juice and purée; continue to cook 25 minutes. Season to taste and garnish with parsley sprigs. Serves 8.

## SWEDISH RICE PORRIDGE

*Photograph on page 47*

2 cups rice
2 tablespoons butter
2 quarts milk
2 teaspoons salt
2 tablespoons sugar
1 small piece stick cinnamon
1 blanched whole almond

Stir rice into 2 cups boiling water, cover and cook over low heat until water is absorbed. Heat butter and milk in a large saucepan. Add salt, sugar and cinnamon; cook over low heat 5 minutes. Stir in partially cooked rice and continue cooking over moderate heat, stirring frequently, about 1 hour. Drop in whole almond just before serving. To serve, pour the porridge into a large bowl and sprinkle the top generously with sugar and ground cinnamon; drop 1 tablespoon butter in center. Spoon into bowls and serve with cold milk, extra cinnamon and sugar. Serves 8.

## TORTELLINI IN BRODO

*Photograph on page 47*

*3 cups flour*
*¾ teaspoon salt*
*4 eggs, well beaten*
*¼ cup grated Parmesan cheese*
*2 tablespoons butter*
*1 Italian sweet sausage, cooked and minced*
*½ cup cooked minced chicken*
*⅛ teaspoon pepper*
*⅛ teaspoon nutmeg*
*2 egg yolks*
*2 quarts seasoned chicken broth*

Mix flour and salt. On a large pastry board make a well in the flour and into this pour the beaten eggs. With a spoon, or hands, slowly mix flour and eggs, working in from point closest to the liquid. More flour or water may be added—the consistency should be such that it can be rolled out ⅛ inch thick.. Knead until smooth and elastic. Let stand 15 minutes. Sprinkle board lightly with flour and, using about ⅓ of the pasta dough at a time, roll it very thin and cut in 2-inch squares. Combine the remaining ingredients, except chicken broth, and mix well. Mixture should be almost a paste when ready for use. Shape the meat mixture into small balls, and place one on each square of dough; brush edges with water and fold over into a triangle. Press edges firmly together, bring two corners of triangle together to form circle, pressing ends together into *tortellini* shape, which is like that of a fortune cookie. Spread the *tortellini* on a floured cloth and let stand overnight to dry. Bring chicken broth to a boil, add *tortellini*. Reduce to moderate heat and cook 20 minutes. Sprinkle with parsley and serve with additional grated Parmesan cheese. Serves 8.

# SEAFOOD

## SHRIMP IN SHERRY SAUCE

*Photograph on page 49*

*1 large garlic clove, 1 teaspoon salt*
*Generous pinch saffron, 1 pinch ground clove*
*1 cup dry sherry*
*3 pounds shrimp, shelled and cleaned*
*⅓ cup olive oil, 1 large sweet onion, chopped*
*3 tablespoons minced parsley*
*1 cup canned pimientos, drained and chopped*
*¼ cup fresh white bread crumbs*

Crush together garlic, salt, saffron and clove. Stir into sherry and let stand 1 hour, then strain. Sauté shrimp in hot oil for 5 minutes; remove from pan. To same oil, add onion, parsley and pimientos; simmer few minutes until onion is soft. Combine sherry, bread crumbs and 1 cup of water in pan, simmer over low heat until sauce is thickened, 8-10 minutes. Add shrimp and heat through. Serve with rice flavored with stewed tomatoes and with a green salad. Serves 8.

## LUTFISK

*Photograph on page 49*

*3 pounds lutfisk, cleaned*
*Salt*
*Mustard Sauce:*
*1½ cups beef stock*
*1 tablespoon dry brown mustard*
*1 tablespoon vinegar*
*1 teaspoon sugar*
*1 teaspoon cornstarch*
*½ teaspoon salt*
*¼ teaspoon white pepper*
*¼ teaspoon paprika*

Wash and skin fish, cut into several large pieces. Place the pieces close together on a piece of cheesecloth and sprinkle with salt; wrap loosely and place on rack in large kettle. Add water to cover and bring to a boil over moderate heat. Reduce heat and simmer for 20 minutes or until tender. Drain and arrange on a warm platter. Serve hot with melted butter and white sauce or mustard sauce. Surround with little boiled potatoes and cooked green peas. Serves 8.
*Mustard Sauce*
Use a wire whisk to combine all ingredients thoroughly, heat to boiling, stirring constantly. As soon as mixture is slightly thickened, strain and serve. Yields about 1 ½ cups.

## PASTA WITH CLAMS

*Photograph on page 49*

*4 dozen littleneck or cherrystone clams*
*2 pounds fettuccelle or other pasta*
*3 garlic cloves*
*¾ cup olive oil*
*6 tablespoons chopped parsley*
*Salt and pepper*
*Butter*

Thoroughly scrub clams, then place in a kettle of cold water for about 1 hour. Drop pasta into boiling salted water and cook 8 to 12 minutes. Drain and keep warm on serving dish. Sauté garlic in hot oil; discard garlic and add drained clams. Cover and steam over medium heat about 5 minutes, or until all the clams open. Add parsley, salt and pepper; cover and steam 2-3 minutes more. Remove clams from sauce and arrange around pasta; strain sauce and pour over pasta, then dot with bits of butter. Serve at once with green salad. Serves 8.

## CHRISTMAS CARP

*Photograph on page 49*

*1 large fresh carp, about 4-5 pounds*
*Stuffing*
*Melted butter*
*1 onion, chopped, ½ cup celery, chopped*
*1 parsley root, diced*
*Peel of ½ lemon, 1 bay leaf, 3-4 peppercorns,*
*2-3 cloves, 1 teaspoon salt*
*1 pint dark beer, 2 cups dry red wine*
*1 cup crumbled gingersnaps, ¼ cup raisins*
Stuffing for Baked Carp
*½ cup fresh rye or pumpernickel bread crumbs*
*1 egg, ¼ cup melted butter*
*1 teaspoon minced onion, 1 tablespoon minced parsley,*
*⅛ teaspoon nutmeg*

Have fish scaled and cleaned. Combine ingredients for stuffing and fill cavity; sew or skewer to close opening. Brush fish with melted butter and place on a greased pan. Bake in a hot oven (400°) 15 minutes. Meanwhile, combine remaining ingredients (except gingersnaps and raisins), bring to a boil and continue cooking over high heat 10 minutes. Reduce heat and keep liquid at a simmer; start basting fish with hot liquid at end of first 15 minutes in oven. Baste fish frequently until done, allowing about 12 minutes for each pound; remove to a hot platter and surround with sauerkraut and potato dumplings. Scrape pan juices into simmering liquid and add gingersnaps; cook few minutes until slightly thickened. Strain liquid, pushing through as much of the soft vegetable pulp as possible; add raisins and cook 2-3 minutes. Serve over fish, or separately for use according to taste. Serves 8.

# ENTREES

## ROAST TURKEY

*Photograph on page 51*

*1 turkey (12-14 pounds ready-to-cook)*
*Stuffing (page 68)*
*⅓ pound boiled ham, thinly sliced*
*⅓ pound salt pork, thinly sliced*

Have turkey cleaned and trussed; loosely stuff neck and body cavities and secure with pins or skewers. Lay ham and salt pork slices over and around bird, securing with pins or thread if necessary. Place turkey, breast up, on a rack in a shallow open pan. Roast in slow oven (325°) for about 5 hours, or until done. Begin by basting bird with a little melted butter or salad oil, continue basting with pan juices as they accumulate. When turkey has been roasting for about 4 hours, remove ham and pork. Serve with mashed potatoes and artichokes or peas. Serves 8-10 with plenty for leftovers.

## ROAST GOOSE

*Photograph on page 53*

*1 goose (10-12 pounds ready to cook)*
*Salt*
*Lemon juice*
*Stuffing (page 68)*

Rub goose inside and out with salt and lemon juice. Let stand 1 hour. Stuff neck and body cavities and pin or sew to close. Bird need not be trussed. Place bird on a rack in a roasting pan. Add 1 cup warm water, cover and let steam over moderate heat about 45 minutes, or until fat in pan begins to sizzle. Prick the skin to release more fat, then place, uncovered, in slow oven (325°) for about 4 hours, or until done. Remove bird to a warm platter and surround with potato dumplings and red cabbage cooked with apples and onions. Serves 8-10.

## CAPPONE ALLA PIGNOLI

*Photograph on page 53*

1 6- to 7-pound capon
1 garlic clove, split
½ teaspoon salt, ¼ teaspoon pepper
1 teaspoon minced parsley
1 tablespoon minced onion
1 tablespoon vinegar
Stuffing (below)
¼ cup olive oil, ¼ cup butter
1 cup pignolia nuts

Rub bird with split garlic clove. Mash together garlic, seasonings, vinegar. Spread paste on damp cheesecloth or toweling. Wrap bird in prepared cloth and let stand 3-4 hours. Remove cloth and wipe away any adhering seasoning paste. Stuff and truss bird; place breast side up in a shallow open roasting pan. Roast in a slow oven (325°) about 4 hours. Melt butter, add olive oil and baste frequently with mixture. Serve on hot platter and garnish with extra pignolias, lemon cups and parsley. Goes well with sweet potato casserole, creamed onions and artichoke hearts. Serves 8.

## CHRISTMAS HAM

*Photograph on page 53*

1 10-12 pound corned ham*
1 tablespoon allspice
2 bay leaves
1 cup brown sugar
1 egg white
1 tablespoon dry mustard
Fine bread crumbs
1 3-ounce package cream cheese
Colored sugars
Fruit garnish

Place ham in a large kettle, fat side up, and cover with cold water; bring to a boil. Skim liquid, add spices and ¼ cup brown sugar. Reduce heat and simmer ham 4 hours or until tender. Skin ham, removing most of fat at same time; return to liquid and let cool. When ham is cold, drain and wipe with paper towels. Beat egg white with mustard and remaining brown sugar. Spread mixture over ham and sprinkle with crumbs. Bake in a moderate oven (350°) 25 minutes or until golden brown. Whip cream cheese with a tablespoon or so of water and put through pastry tube to decorate ham; sprinkle with varicolored sugars. Garnish platter with cooked prunes, apple rings, lingonberries and parsley. Serve with glazed carrots, applesauce with prunes, and creamed potatoes seasoned with a touch of nutmeg. Serves 8 to 10.

* If corned ham is not available in your market, your butcher will put one down for you, but should have about 2 weeks notice. Or use a regular smoked ham and prepare as directed.

## STUFFINGS

*Photograph on page 54*

Spanish Stuffing
for Turkey:
10 slices firm white bread, crusts removed
6 slices bacon, diced, 1 small onion, minced
Turkey heart and liver, boiled and chopped
1 tablespoon minced parsley
2 tablespoons butter
1 black truffle, minced
10 large stuffed olives, chopped
2 eggs, beaten, salt and pepper

Stuffing for Capon:
Capon giblets
2 links sweet Italian sausage
2 tablespoons olive oil, 1 egg
1 tablespoon minced parsley
1 cup day-old bread cubes
6 boiled chestnuts, mashed
2 tablespoons butter

Stuffing for Goose:
8 slices day-old bread, 1 cup milk
1 cup chopped onion, 1 tablespoon minced parsley
2 tablespoons butter, cooked heart and liver, minced
2 eggs separated, 1 apple, chopped, salt and pepper
⅛ teaspoon nutmeg, ½ teaspoon dried sage

*Spanish Stuffing for Turkey*
Toast bread until very hard and well browned; break into a bowl and add boiling water to cover; let stand. In a skillet, combine bacon, onion, heart, liver, parsley and butter. Stir over moderate heat 10 minutes. Drain and mash soaked toast, then combine all ingredients and mix well, seasoning to taste. If desired, a leaf or two of sage may be added. Makes enough for a 12-pound turkey.

*Stuffing for Capon*
Mince giblets, skin and cut up sausages. Sauté together in hot oil. Combine all ingredients and mix well. If necessary, mix in 1 or 2 tablespoons boiling water to blend and lighten. Enough for 1 capon.

*Stuffing for Goose*
Soak bread in milk; press dry and crumble. Cook onion and parsley in hot butter 3 minutes; stir in bread pulp. Mix heart and liver with egg yolks and apple. Combine 2 mixtures and add seasoning. Beat egg whites until stiff, fold into stuffing mixture. Enough to stuff neck and body cavities of 10-12 pound goose.

# DESSERTS

## OLD-FASHIONED PLUM PUDDING

*Photograph on page 57*

*½ cup fine dry crumbs*
*1 cup hot milk*
*4 eggs*
*¾ cup brown sugar*
*1 cup brandy*
*½ pound minced beef suet*
*1 cup flour*
*1 teaspoon salt*
*1 teaspoon nutmeg*
*¼ teaspoon ground cloves*
*½ teaspoon cinnamon*
*¼ teaspoon mace*
*1 cup seedless raisins*
*1 cup chopped candied cherries*
*2 cups diced glacéed fruit*
*½ cup chopped walnuts*

Combine crumbs and milk, let stand. Beat eggs with sugar and half the brandy; stir mixtures together and add suet. Combine flour, salt and spices in a sifter; sift over fruit and nuts mixed in a large bowl. Mix thoroughly, then blend in crumb-suet mixture and remaining brandy. Turn the mixture into a greased 2-quart round-bottomed bowl and cover tightly with a doubled piece of heavy foil. Place mold on a rack in a deep kettle and add hot water to about half the depth of the mold. Cover kettle and steam for about 4 hours, adding more hot water as it boils away. Take mold from water and remove foil; bake in a slow oven (325°) about 45 minutes, or until top is dried and firm. If pudding is to be stored to ripen before using, leave in mold, wrap and place in a cool dark place for a month or more. If pudding is to be served at once, turn out of bowl and spoon heated brandy over top. Serve aflame. Serves 8-10.

## MINCEMEAT PIE

*Photograph on page 57*

*1 pound lean beef*
*½ pound beef suet*
*4 tart apples, peeled and chopped*
*1 cup granulated sugar*
*1 cup brown sugar, ¼ cup molasses*
*2 cups cider or apple juice*
*1 pound currants, 1 pound raisins*
*¼ pound citron, thinly sliced*
*1 lemon, seeded and ground*
*¾ teaspoon mace, ¾ teaspoon nutmeg*
*¾ teaspoon cloves*
*¾ teaspoon allspice*
*1 teaspoon cinnamon*
*1 teaspoon salt*
*1 cup whiskey or brandy*

*Pie Pastry:*
*2 cups flour*
*2 egg yolks*
*2-3 tablespoons sugar*
*1 cup butter*
*½ teaspoon salt*
*1 tablespoon grated lemon rind*

Have butcher grind beef and suet together. In a large heavy saucepan, mix ground meat and fat with apples, sugars, molasses and cider. Bring to a boil. Stir in fruit, reduce heat and cook for about 1 hour, stirring often to prevent sticking. Add the spices and salt and continue cooking until very thick, stirring continuously. Stir in the whiskey or brandy and pack mixture into prepared jars. Adjust lids and process in hot water bath for 1½ hours. Seal, cool and store. Makes about 5 pints.

*Pie Pastry*

Sift the flour into a large mixing bowl. Make a well in the center and add remaining ingredients. Mix center ingredients, then use a pastry blender or fork to work in the flour. If necessary, work in 2 tablespoons cold water to pull dough into a ball. Wrap and chill 1 hour.

Roll out pastry and fit gently into 9-inch flan ring set on cookie sheet. Trim off excess pastry. Fill with 3 or 4 cups mincemeat, depending on thickness of pie desired. Gather together and reroll bits of leftover pastry and use to make top edge of pie, also leaf and berry cutouts for decoration. Bake in a hot oven (400°) 40 to 50 minutes or until crust is a golden brown. Cool before removing ring. Makes 8-10 servings.

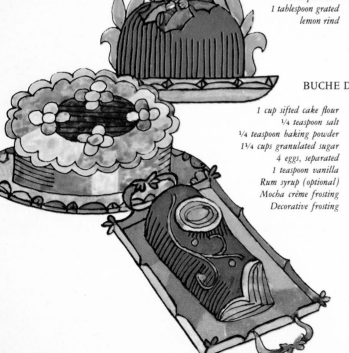

## BUCHE DE NOEL

*Photograph on page 57*

*1 cup sifted cake flour*
*¼ teaspoon salt*
*¼ teaspoon baking powder*
*1¼ cups granulated sugar*
*4 eggs, separated*
*1 teaspoon vanilla*
*Rum syrup (optional)*
*Mocha crème frosting*
*Decorative frosting*

Combine dry ingredients, using half the sugar. Sift together twice. Beat egg whites until stiff and peaky, then gradually beat in the remaining sugar. Beat egg yolks until thick and light, add vanilla and fold gently into beaten egg whites. Lightly fold in flour mixture, about 3-4 table-spoons at a time. Pour the batter into a wax-paper-lined 15-x-10-x-1-inch jelly-roll pan and spread evenly. Bake in a hot oven (400°) about 15 minutes, or until cake is a light brown and firm to the touch. Loosen the cake with a spatula and turn out onto a clean dish towel lightly dusted with confectioners' sugar. Pull off wax paper and use kitchen shears to trim off crusty edges. Starting from narrow end, roll up cake and towel together. Cool for 15 minutes. Unroll, brush cake with rum syrup if used, and spread with mocha crème frosting. Roll as for jelly roll, again start-ing at narrow end and shaping firmly. Wrap and chill 4 hours. When fill-ing is very firm, brush cake with rum syrup (if used), and cut several diagonal pieces from end for use as "knots" and "branches" when decorating. Frost the cake with mocha crème, using a serrated tube and running the frosting in lengthwise strips to look like bark. Press the "knots" and "branches" firmly into applied frosting and frost with more mocha crème. Finish the ends of the "log," "branches," etc., with light coffee-colored decorative icing, spreading roughly with a spatula to give a cut appearance. Decorate the log as desired, using decorative frosting in appropriate colors to make holly, ivy, etc. To keep frosting firm, chill until ready to serve. Makes 8-10 servings. *Rum Syrup:* In a saucepan combine and simmer for 5 minutes ½ cup water, ½ cup sugar, 1 thin slice lemon, 1 small piece stick cinnamon, ½ teaspoon vanilla. Stir in ¼ cup rum, strain and use hot.

**Mocha Crème Frosting**

*1⅓ cups granulated sugar*
*4 egg yolks*
*1 pound butter*
*2 squares unsweetened chocolate, melted*
*1 tablespoon instant coffee*
*2 tablespoons rum*

*Mocha Crème Frosting*

Boil sugar with ½ cup water to the soft-ball stage (240° on candy thermometer). Beat egg yolks until thick and light and continue beating while gradually adding the hot syrup. When all the syrup has been added, continue beating mixture until it is cold. Have the butter at room temperature and beat into mixture about ¼ cup at a time. Beat in remaining ingredients. If working in a warm room, keep frosting firm by setting bowl in a pan of ice cubes. Makes enough to fill and frost Christmas log.

**Decorative Frosting**

*½ cup vegetable shortening*
*2 tablespoons butter*
*2 cups sifted confectioners' sugar*
*½ teaspoon vanilla*

*Decorative Frosting*

Cream shortening and butter, beat in confectioners' sugar and vanilla. Beat until smooth and stiff enough to put through pastry tube. Frosting will be a creamy white; divide and color for decorating log.

---

# SWEET BREADS

## CHRISTMAS BREAD DOUGH

*4 packages activated yeast*
*1 teaspoon salt*
*½ cup sugar*
*7 egg yolks or 3 whole eggs*
*1 teaspoon vanilla*
*½ teaspoon grated lemon rind*
*4 to 5 cups flour*
*½ cup butter, softened*

Dissolve yeast in 1 cup lukewarm water, add salt and sugar. Stir in eggs, vanilla and lemon rind. Add enough flour to make a soft dough. Work in butter. Add more flour if needed. Knead dough on floured surface for 10 minutes or until it is shiny and elastic. Place in a floured bowl. Dust the top lightly with flour. Cover bowl with a towel. Place in a draft-free place to rise for 30 minutes, or until dough doubles in bulk. (The inside of an unlighted oven is ideal.) Dough has risen enough if it does not spring back when fingers are poked into the center. Punch the dough down. Knead it briefly. Dough will keep up to four days in a covered container in the refrigerator. At first, it may need punching down every hour or two—so don't make dough at night. Once thoroughly cold, it needs to be punched down once a day. This dough is used in all the following recipes for sweet breads.

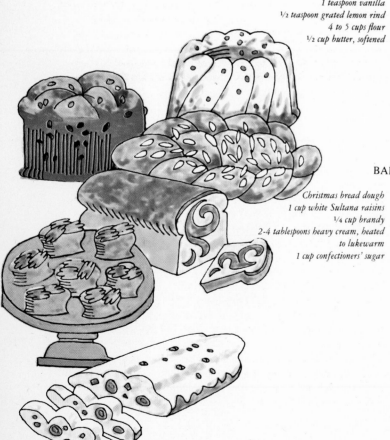

## BABKA

*Photograph on pages 58-59*

*Christmas bread dough*
*1 cup white Sultana raisins*
*¼ cup brandy*
*2-4 tablespoons heavy cream, heated to lukewarm*
*1 cup confectioners' sugar*

Let dough rise until doubled in bulk. Grease one 10-inch or two 7-inch gugelhupf pans. Punch dough down, work in raisins. Fill pan half full. Let dough rise in pan until it doubles again. Bake in moderate oven (375°) 45 minutes for 10-inch size, 30 minutes for 7-inch size, or until deep brown. Remove from pan. Sprinkle with brandy. Add enough cream to sugar to make a thin icing. Brush on warm *babka*.

## HUNGARIAN NUT ROLL

*Photograph on pages 58-59*

*Christmas bread dough*
*2 eggs, 2/3 cup sugar*
*1 cup walnuts or pecans, grated*
*1/2 cup white raisins*
*1/3 cup melted butter*
*1 teaspoon grated orange rind*
*1 teaspoon vanilla, 1 egg white*
*1 teaspoon ground cinnamon*

Grease two 9x5x3-inch loaf pans. Roll dough into a rectangle 1/4 inch thick. Beat eggs and 1/3 cup sugar until fluffy. Add nuts, raisins, butter, orange rind and vanilla. Spread mixture over dough. Roll up, jelly-roll style. Cut in half. Fit each half into a pan. Let rise until almost doubled in bulk. Brush with egg white mixed with 1 teaspoon water. Sprinkle with 1/3 cup sugar mixed with cinnamon. Bake in moderate oven (350°) for 45 minutes or until deep brown.

## ORANGE HONEY BRAID

*Photograph on pages 58-59*

*Christmas bread dough*
*1/2 cup butter*
*1/2 cup honey*
*1 teaspoon grated orange rind*
*1/2 teaspoon ground cardamom*
*1 cup finely chopped walnuts*
*1 cup white raisins*
*1/2 cup diced candied orange peel*
*2 egg yolks, beaten*
*2 teaspoons light cream*
*1/2 cup blanched sliced almonds*

Grease a large cookie sheet. Roll dough into a square 1/4 inch thick. Cream the butter, honey, orange rind and cardamom together. Spread mixture evenly over dough, then scatter walnuts, raisins and orange peel on top. Roll up loosely, jelly-roll style. Flatten out filled dough with a rolling pin to make it no more than 1 inch thick. Cut it lengthwise into six equal strips. Using three strips for each set, plait them together to make two braids. Pinch the ends of the braids together. Place them well apart on cookie sheet. Let braids rise until doubled in bulk. Brush with egg yolks mixed with cream. Sprinkle with sliced almonds. Bake in moderate oven (350°) for 45 minutes or until braids are golden brown.

## SCHNECKEN

*Photograph on pages 58-59*

*Christmas bread dough*
*1/2 cup soft butter*
*1 1/2 cups light-brown sugar, packed*
*1 tablespoon white corn syrup*
*2 cups pecan halves*
*1 cup currants*
*1 cup finely ground pecans*
*2 teaspoons ground cinnamon*

Cream butter with 1/2 cup sugar. Beat in corn syrup. Grease cups of two 24-muffin tins with mixture. Place pecan halves in muffin cups. Roll dough into a long rectangle 1/4 inch thick. Sprinkle with 1 cup sugar and the currants, ground pecans and cinnamon. Roll up dough tightly, pressing seam closed, to make a long roll about the diameter of the muffin cups. Slice roll into pieces which will half fill depth of cups. Place slices in cups and press down firmly. Let rise only until the dough looks puffy. Bake in moderate oven (375°) for 10 minutes or until brown. Turn pans upside down on cake rack immediately to remove *schnecken* from cups and to allow sugar-syrup to run over sides. Makes 4 dozen.

## PANETTONE

*Photograph on pages 58-59*

*Christmas bread dough*
*1/2 cup white raisins*
*1/2 cup dark raisins*
*1/2 cup diced candied citron*
*1/2 cup melted butter*

Grease two deep, round 8-inch pans. Cut two collars from heavy brown paper to make each pan about 9 inches high. Grease collars and fasten with pins and string. Let dough rise once, knead in raisins and citron. Shape dough into two balls. Place one in each pan, cut a cross on top. Let rise until almost double. Brush with butter. Bake in hot oven (400°) for 10 minutes. Reduce heat to 350°. Bake for 30 minutes or until brown, brushing twice more with butter.

## STOLLEN

*Photograph on pages 58-59*

*Christmas bread dough*
*3/4 cup white raisins*
*1/2 cup currants*
*1 cup mixed, diced candied fruit*
*1/4 cup brandy*
*1/3 cup blanched, sliced almonds, lightly toasted*
*Melted butter*
*Confectioners' sugar*

Mix fruit and brandy. Let stand 1 hour. Drain excess liquid, knead fruit and almonds into dough. Lightly grease a large baking sheet. Cut dough in half. Roll each piece into an oval 1/3 inch thick. Fold each oval so that bottom edge extends beyond the top. Roll lightly to set fold. Place ovals well apart on baking sheet. Let rise only until puffy. Brush with butter. Bake in moderate oven (375°) for 45 minutes or until brown. Brush with butter while hot, and again after cakes cool. Dust with sugar. Before serving, sugar again.

# COOKIES

## SUGAR COOKIES

*Photograph on page 61*

*1 cup butter*
*2 cups confectioners' sugar*
*2 eggs*
*2 tablespoons whiskey*
*1/2 teaspoon vanilla*
*3 cups flour*
*1/4 teaspoon nutmeg*
*1/4 teaspoon salt*

Cream butter and sugar, add eggs one at a time and beat smooth. Mix whiskey and vanilla. Combine and sift dry ingredients. Alternately add liquid and dry ingredients to creamed mixture, blending smooth each time. Chill for 2-3 hours, or until dough is stiff enough to handle. Roll out about one third of dough at a time on lightly floured board. Cut into bells, stars, angels, etc. Place on ungreased cookie sheets and brush with egg white beaten with a little water. Sprinkle with sugar. Bake in a moderate oven (350°) 12-15 minutes. Makes 5-6 dozen cookies.

## PASTINI DI NATALE

*Photograph on page 61*

*3 cups flour*
*1/2 teaspoon salt*
*2 teaspoons baking powder*
*1 cup butter*
*1 1/4 cup sugar*
*2 eggs*
*1 lemon rind, grated*
*1/4 cup pistachio nuts, minced*

Sift dry ingredients in a bowl, cut in butter until mixture resembles coarse corn meal. Beat sugar with eggs and lemon rind, add to flour mixture. Mix until ingredients hold together, then knead or mix in nuts. Shape into a ball, wrap and chill 1 hour. Using about one third of dough at a time, roll out 1/4 inch thick on lightly floured board. Cut into holiday shapes. Place on ungreased cookie sheets and bake in a hot oven (425°) 10 minutes, or until light brown. Makes about 3 dozen cookies.

## ZUCKER HUTCHEN

*Photograph on page 61*

*1/2 cup soft butter, 1/2 cup sugar*
*1 egg yolk, 2 tablespoons milk*
*1 1/2 cups flour*
*1/2 teaspoon baking powder*
*1/4 teaspoon salt*
*1/3 cup finely cut-up citron*
Meringue Frosting:
*1 egg white*
*1 1/2 cups sifted confectioners' sugar*
*1/4 teaspoon vanilla*
*1/2 cup chopped almonds*

Cream together butter, sugar and egg yolk, stir in milk. Combine and sift dry ingredients, stir into butter mixture. Mix in citron. Chill dough 2-3 hours. Roll out on a floured board and cut into rounds. Heap 1 teaspoon meringue frosting in center of each round and top with a candied cherry. Place on greased cookie sheet and bake in moderate oven (350°) 10-12 minutes. Makes about 4 dozen cookies. *Meringue Frosting:* Beat egg white until frothy. Gradually beat in sugar and vanilla. Beat until frosting holds peaks, stir in chopped almonds.

## GEBACKENES

*Photograph on page 61*

*2 cups flour*
*1/2 teaspoon baking powder*
*1/8 teaspoon cinnamon*
*1/2 cup soft butter, 1 cup sugar*
*1/4 cup evaporated milk, 1 egg, beaten*
*1/2 teaspoon vanilla*
*1 tablespoon brandy*

Sift together dry ingredients. Cream until thick butter, sugar, milk and egg. Combine 2 mixtures, add vanilla and mix until smooth. Chill overnight. Using about one third of dough at a time, roll out on lightly floured board and cut into birds and other fancy shapes. Place on ungreased cookie sheet and brush with brandy. Bake in moderate oven (375°) 15-18 minutes or until done. Makes about 6 dozen cookies.

## CHRISTMAS COOKIES

*Photograph on page 61*

*1/3 cup soft butter*
*1/3 cup sugar, 1 egg*
*2/3 cup light honey*
*2 3/4 cups flour*
*1 teaspoon soda, 1 teaspoon salt*
*1/2 teaspoon vanilla*
*1/2 teaspoon lemon extract*

Thoroughly mix butter, sugar, egg and honey. Combine and sift dry ingredients, stir into butter mixture. Add flavorings. Blend well to make a smooth dough. Chill 2-3 hours. Roll dough 1/4 inch thick on lightly floured board; cut into all kinds of holiday and tree-ornament shapes. Place on lightly greased cookie sheets and bake in moderate oven (375°) 8-10 minutes. Makes about 5 dozen cookies.

## SPECULAAS

*Photograph on page 61*

*2 1/2 cups flour*
*1/2 teaspoon salt*
*1/2 teaspoon baking powder*
*1 teaspoon cinnamon, 1/8 teaspoon crushed cardamom*
*1/2 cup butter*
*1 cup confectioners' sugar, 1 egg*
*1 tablespoon grated lemon rind*

Sift together dry ingredients. Cream butter and sugar. Beat egg and lemon rind into creamed mixture, then add dry ingredients and mix well. Chill dough for 2-3 hours, or until firm enough to handle easily. Roll out on lightly floured board and cut into trees, rounds and other shapes. Place on greased cookie sheets and bake in a moderate oven (350°) 12-15 minutes. Makes about 8 dozen cookies.

## SPRITZKUCHEN

*Photograph on page 61*

*1 cup butter*
*¾ cup sugar*
*1 egg*
*½ teaspoon almond extract*
*2½ cups flour*

Cream butter and sugar, blend in egg and flavoring. Mix in flour. Put dough through a cookie press in fancy and holiday shapes. Form cookies directly on cold, ungreased cookie sheets. Bake in a hot oven (425°) about 12-15 minutes. Makes about 6 dozen cookies.

## EIER KRINGEL

*Photograph on page 61*

*¾ cup butter*
*1 cup granulated sugar*
*3 raw egg yolks*
*4 cooked egg yolks, sieved*
*1 lemon rind, grated*
*½ teaspoon mace*
*½ teaspoon vanilla*
*3 cups flour*

Cream the butter and sugar until light and fluffy. Beat in 2 raw egg yolks, the sieved egg yolks, rind, mace and vanilla. Use hands to work in the flour, 1 cup at a time. Dough should be very stiff; if necessary work in a little more flour. Smooth out dough by kneading for 3 or 4 minutes. Chill 1 hour. Roll out ¼ inch thick on a floured board, cut wreath shape with a doughnut cutter. Place on very lightly greased cookie sheets and brush with remaining raw egg yolk beaten with a little cold water. Sprinkle with sugar. Bake in a slow oven (325°) about 15 minutes or until a pale golden color. Makes about 6 dozen wreaths.

## SPICE COOKIES

*Photograph on page 61*

*½ cup light molasses*
*½ cup shortening*
*⅓ cup light-brown sugar*
*1 teaspoon cinnamon, ½ teaspoon ground cloves*
*½ teaspoon ginger, 1 teaspoon grated lemon rind*
*1 teaspoon baking soda, 1 teaspoon vanilla*
*2½ cups flour*

In a saucepan combine and bring to boil molasses, shortening and sugar. Cook until sugar is melted, then mix in spices, lemon rind, baking soda and vanilla. Cool to room temperature, gradually beat in flour. Chill for 1 hour, or until firm enough to handle. Roll out on floured board and cut into bird and animal shapes. Place on greased cookie sheets and bake in a moderate oven (350°) 6-8 minutes or until done. Makes about 6 dozen cookies.

---

# TOASTS

## CELERY BOWL

*Photograph on page 63*

*1 bunch celery*
*1 cup sugar*
*1 cup light rum*
*2 bottles Moselle wine, chilled*

Clean celery and slice into a bowl. Wrap leaves and store in refrigerator. To celery add sugar, rum and 1 cup water; stir until sugar dissolves, then chill until ready to use. To serve, strain liquid into a pitcher and stir in wine. Decorate with celery leaves and serve at once. Yields about 2 quarts.

## TOM AND JERRY

*Photograph on page 63*

*12 eggs*
*1 pound sugar*
*½ cup Jamaica rum*
*3 cups bourbon*
*Nutmeg*

Beat the eggs until very thick and light; gradually add sugar and continue beating until mixture resembles a thick batter. Stir in rum and whiskey; let stand 3 hours to ripen flavors. To serve, spoon several tablespoons of mixture into individual cup or mug; stir in boiling water to taste and sprinkle with nutmeg. Yields about 2 quarts.

## CHRISTMAS CAROL PUNCH

*Photograph on page 63*

*½ to ¾ cup sugar*
*½ cup lemon juice*
*½ pint ginger brandy, 1 bottle Jamaica rum*
*6 cinnamon sticks, 2 tablespoons whole cloves*
*1 thinly sliced orange, 1 thinly sliced lemon*

Dissolve sugar in 2 cups boiling water; add lemon juice, brandy, rum and spices. Simmer 10 minutes, then pour into punch bowl. Garnish with fruit slices and serve hot. Yields about 2 quarts.

## GLOGG

*Photograph on page 63*

*1 bottle claret, 1 bottle port*
*2 tablespoons diced candied orange peels*
*10 cardamom seeds*
*3 small pieces stick cinnamon*
*2 tablespoons whole cloves*
*½ pound blanched almonds*
*½ pound seedless raisins*
*½ pound sugar cubes*
*1 pint cognac*

In a large kettle, combine and heat the wines. Tie the peel and whole spices in a square of cheesecloth, add to hot wine and simmer 15 minutes. Add the almonds and raisins; simmer 20 minutes. Remove from heat and discard spice bag. Pile sugar cubes into sieve and hold over kettle; gradually pour the cognac over the sugar, then flame contents of kettle with a match. Ladle the hot burning liquid over the sugar while it melts and drips down to sweeten the glögg. Cover kettle to put out the flame. Serve hot with a few raisins and almonds in each cup. Yields about 2 quarts.

# on lending a punch-bowl

*Oliver Wendell Holmes Sr. (1809-1894), author of "The Autocrat of the Breakfast-Table," here traces the history of a punch bowl that has provided cheer for many generations.*

This ancient silver bowl of mine, it tells of good old
times,
Of joyous days and jolly nights, and merry Christmas times;
They were a free and jovial race, but honest, brave,
and true,
Who dipped their ladle in the punch when this old
bowl was new.

A Spanish galleon brought the bar,—so runs the
ancient tale;
'Twas hammered by an Antwerp smith, whose arm
was like a flail;
And now and then between the strokes, for fear his
strength should fail,
He wiped his brow and quaffed a cup of good old
Flemish ale.
'Twas purchased by an English squire to please his
loving dame,
Who saw the cherubs, and conceived a longing for
the same;
And oft as on the ancient stock another twig was
found,
'Twas filled with candle spiced and hot, and handed
smoking round.

But, changing hands, it reached at length a Puritan
divine,
Who used to follow Timothy, and take a little wine,
But hated punch and prelacy; and so it was, perhaps,
He went to Leyden, where he found conventicles
and schnapps.

And then, of course, you know what's next: it left
the Dutchman's shore
With those that in the Mayflower came,—a hundred
souls and more,—

Along with all the furniture, to fill their new
abodes,—
To judge by what is still on hand, at least a hundred
loads.

'Twas on a dreary winter's eve, the night was closing
dim,
When brave Miles Standish took the bowl, and
filled it to the brim;
The little Captain stood and stirred the posset with
his sword,
And all his sturdy men-at-arms were ranged about
the board.

He poured the fiery Hollands in,—the man that
never feared,—
He took a long and solemn draught, and wiped his
yellow beard;
And one by one the musketeers—the men that
fought and prayed—
All drank as 'twere their mother's milk, and not a
man afraid.

That night, affrighted from his nest, the screaming
eagle flew,
He heard the Pequot's ringing whoop, the soldier's
wild halloo;
And there the sachem learned the rule he taught to
kith and kin,
"Run from the white man when you find he smells
of Hollands gin!"

A hundred years, and fifty more, had spread their
leaves and snows,
A thousand rubs had flattened down each little
cherub's nose,
When once again the bowl was filled, but not in
mirth or joy,—
'Twas mingled by a mother's hand to cheer her
parting boy.

Drink, John, she said, 'twill do you good,—poor
child, you'll never bear
This working in the dismal trench, out in the midnight air;
And if—God bless me!—you were hurt, 'twould
keep away the chill.
So John *did* drink,—and well he wrought that
night at Bunker's Hill!

I tell you, there was generous warmth in good old
English cheer;
I tell you, 'twas a pleasant thought to bring its
symbol here.
'Tis but the fool that loves excess; hast thou a
drunken soul?

Thy bane is in thy shallow skull, not in my silver
  bowl!

I love the memory of the past,—its pressed yet
  fragrant flowers,—
The moss that clothes its broken walls, the ivy on
  its towers;
Nay, this poor bauble it bequeathed,—my eyes
  grow moist and dim,
To think of all the vanished joys that danced around
  its brim.

Then fill a fair and honest cup, and bear it straight
  to me;
The goblet hallows all it holds, whate'er the liquid
  be;
And may the cherubs on its face protect me from
  the sin
That dooms one to those dreadful words,—"My
  dear, where *have* you been?"

# REGINALD'S REVENGE

*Few guests at the forced gaiety of after-Christ-
mas-dinner festivities have ever acted as badly
as Reginald in this excerpt from the short story.
"Reginald's Christmas Revel," by British author Saki (Hector Hugh Munro, 1870-1916).*

I shall never forget putting in a Christmas at the
Babwolds'. Mrs. Babwold is some relation of my
father's—a sort of to-be-left-till-called-for cousin
—and that was considered sufficient reason for my
having to accept her invitation at about the sixth
time of asking; though why the sins of the father
should be visited by the children . . .

Of course there were other people there. There
was a Major Somebody who had shot things in
Lapland, or somewhere of that sort; I forget what
they were, but it wasn't for want of reminding. We
had them cold with every meal almost, and he was
continually giving us details of what they measured from tip to tip, as though he thought we were
going to make them warm under-things . . .

On Christmas evening we were supposed to be
especially festive in the Old English fashion. The
hall was horribly draughty, but it seemed to be the
proper place to revel in, and it was decorated with
Japanese fans and Chinese lanterns, which gave it
a very Old English effect. A young lady with a con-
fidential voice favoured us with a long recitation
about a little girl who died or did something equal-
ly hackneyed, and then the Major gave us a graphic
account of a struggle he had with a wounded bear.
I privately wished that the bears would win sometimes on these occasions; at least they wouldn't go
vapouring about it afterwards. Before we had time
to recover our spirits, we were indulged with some
thought-reading by a young man whom one knew
instinctively had a good mother and an indiffer-
ent tailor—the sort of young man who talks un-
flaggingly through the thickest soup, and smooths
his hair dubiously as though he thought it might
hit back. The thought-reading was rather a suc-
cess; he announced that the hostess was thinking
about poetry, and she admitted that her mind was
dwelling on one of Austin's odes. Which was near
enough. I fancy she had been really wondering
whether a scrag-end of mutton and some cold
plum-pudding would do for the kitchen dinner
next day. As a crowning dissipation, they all sat
down to play progressive halma, with milk-choco-
late for prizes. I've been carefully brought up, and
I don't like to play games of skill for milk-choco-
late, so I invented a headache and retired from the
scene. I had been preceded a few minutes earlier
by Miss Langshan-Smith, a rather formidable lady,
who always got up at some uncomfortable hour in
the morning, and gave you the impression that she
had been in communication with most of the European Governments before breakfast. There was a
paper pinned on her door with a signed request
that she might be called particularly early on the
morrow. Such an opportunity does not come twice
in a lifetime. I covered up everything except the
signature with another notice, to the effect that before these words should meet the eye she would
have ended a misspent life, was sorry for the trouble she was giving, and would like a military funeral. A few minutes later I violently exploded an air-
filled paper bag on the landing, and gave a stage
moan that could have been heard in the cellars.
Then I pursued my original intention and went to
bed. The noise those people made in forcing open
the good lady's door was positively indecorous;
she resisted gallantly, but I believe they searched
her for bullets for about a quarter of an hour, as if
she had been a historic battlefield.

I hate traveling on Boxing Day, but one must oc-
casionally do things that one dislikes.

# THE WAY IT USED TO BE

*Robert Benchley was on a diet when he read the Christmas menu of a Chicago hotel. He expressed his envious amazement in this essay.*

I realize as well as anybody that to talk about dieting at this late date is like discussing whether or not the polka causes giddiness or arguing about the merits of the coaster brake on a bicycle. Dieting, as such, is no longer a subject for conversation.

But the whole question has been brought to my mind with a fresh crash by the finding of an old menu among my souvenirs (several of the souvenirs I cannot quite make out—even if I knew what they were, I can see no reason for having saved them), an old menu of a Christmas dinner dispensed to the guests of a famous Chicago hotel in the year 1885. I was not exactly in a position to be eating a dinner like this in 1885, but some of my kind relatives had saved it for my torture . . .

The dinner was, of course, table d'hôte. When you bought a dinner in those days, you bought a *dinner*. None of this skimming over the card and saying, "I don't see anything I want. Just bring me an alligator-pear salad." If you couldn't see anything you wanted on one of the old-fashioned table d'hôte menus, you just couldn't see, that's all . . .

After the customary blue-points and soup, with a comparatively meager assortment of fish (just a stuffed black bass and boiled salmon), we find a choice of broiled leg of mountain sheep or wild turkey. This is just as a starter. The boys didn't get down to business until the roast. There are thirty-six choices among the roasts. Among the more distinguished names listed were:

Leg of moose, loin of elk, cinnamon bear, black-tail deer, loin of venison, saddle of antelope (the National Geographic Society evidently did the shopping for meat in behalf of this hotel), opossum, black bear, and then the duck.

The duck will have to have a paragraph all by itself. In fact, we may have to build a small house for it. When this chef came to the duck, he just threw his apron over his head and said: "I'm going crazy, boys—don't stop me!" He had canvasback duck, wood duck, butterball duck, brant, mallard duck, blue-winged teal, spoonbill duck, sage hen, green-winged teal, and pintail duck, to say nothing of partridge, quail, plover, and some other of the cheap birds.

I am not quite sure what a sage hen is, and I doubt very much if I should have ordered it on that Christmas Day, but *some*body thought enough of it to go out and snare two or three just in case, and it seems to me that this is the spirit that has made America what it is today . . .

So, after toying with all the members of the duck family except decoys and clay pigeons, the diner of 1885 cast his eye down the card to what were called "Broiled," a very simple, honest name for what followed. Teal duck (evidently one of the teal ducks from the roast column slipped down into the broiled, and liked it so well that it stayed), ricebirds, marsh birds, sand snipe, reedbirds, blackbirds, and red-winged starling . . .

By this time you would have supposed that they had used up all the birds within a radius of 3,000 miles of Chicago, leaving none to wake people up in the morning. But no. Among the entrées they must have a fillet of pheasant *financière*, which certainly must have come as a surprise to the dinner parties and tasted good after all that broiled pheasant and roast pheasant. Nothing tastes so good after a broiled pheasant as a good fillet of pheasant *financière* . . .

There then seemed to have come over the chef a feeling that he wasn't doing quite the right thing by his guests. Oh, it had been all right up to this point, but he hadn't really shown what he could do. So he got up a team of what he called "ornamental dishes," and when he said "ornamental" I rather imagine he meant "ornamental." They probably had to be brought in by the town fire department and eaten standing on a ladder. Playing left end for the "ornamental dishes" we find a pyramid of wild turkey in aspic. Perhaps you would like to stop right there. If you did you would miss the aspic of lobster Queen Victoria, and you couldn't really be said to have dined unless you had had aspic of lobster Queen Victoria. I rather imagine that it made quite an impressive ornamental dish—that is, if it looked anything like Queen Victoria . . .

Now the question arises—what did people look like after they had eaten a dinner like that? Were people in 1885 so much fatter than those of us today who go around nibbling at bits of pineapple and drinking sips of sauer-kraut juice? I personally don't remember, but it doesn't seem that people were so much worse off in those days. At any rate, they had a square meal once in a while.

I am not a particularly proud man and it doesn't make an awful lot of difference to anyone whether I am fat or not. But as I don't like to run out of breath when I stoop over to tie my shoes, I try to follow the various bits of advice which people give me in the matter of diet. As a result, I get very little to eat, and am cross and hungry most of the time. I feel like a crook every time I take a furtive forkful of potato, and once, after sneaking a piece of hot bread, I was on the verge of giving myself up to the police as a dangerous character.

Surely there are more noble aspects (aspect of lobster Queen Victoria, for instance) than that of a man who is afraid to take a piece of bread. I am going to get some photographs of people in 1885 and give quite a lot of study to finding out whether they were very much heavier than people today. If I find that they weren't, I am going to take that menu of the Chicago Christmas dinner and get some chef, or organization of chefs, to duplicate it. The worst that can happen to me after eating it will be that I drop dead.

# Here We Come A-Wassailing

*This carol recalls the old English custom of wassailing, when waits went singing from door to door on Christmas Eve. Some of the words date from the 17th Century.*

*Here we come a - was-sail-ing A -mong the leaves so green, Here we come a -*

*wand'- ring, So fair___ to be seen. Love and joy come to you, And to*

*you your was-sail too, And God bless you, and send___ you a hap - - py New*

*Year, And God send you a hap - - py New Year.*

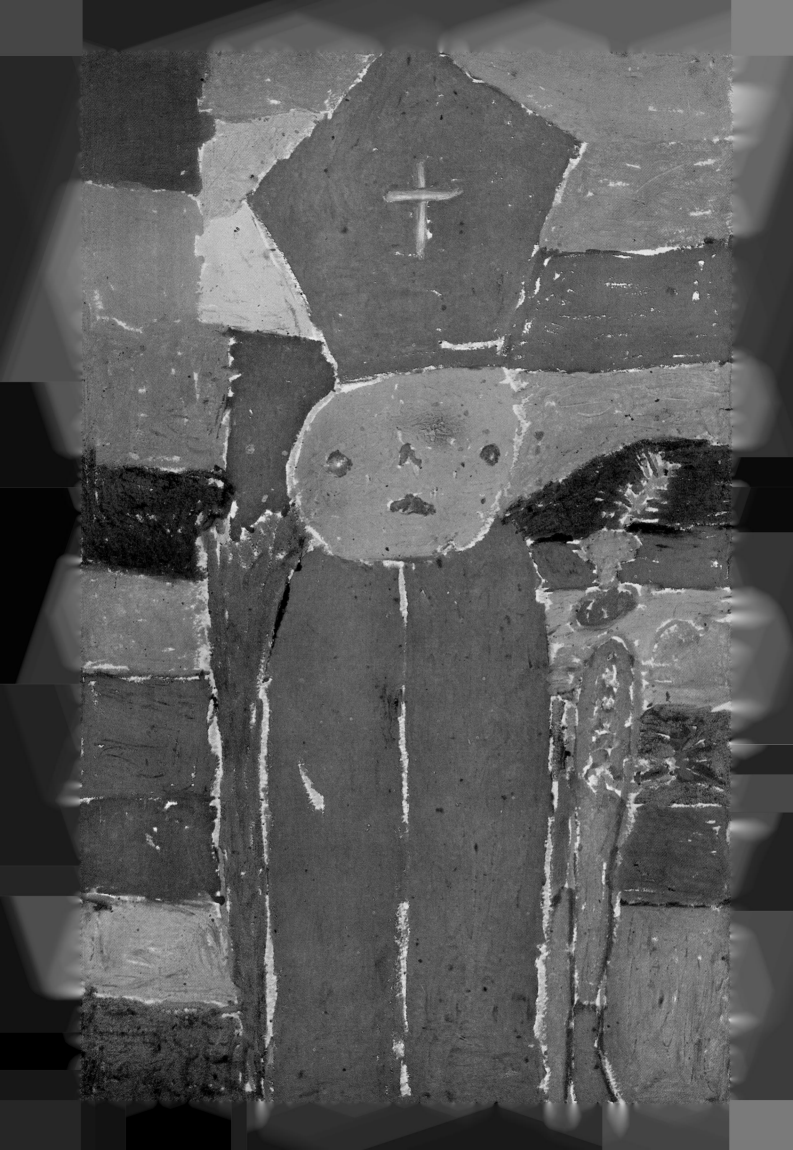

# III

# A CHILDREN'S TREASURY

IT WAS THE MIDDLE OF THE night. And night of all nights it was Christmas. The children couldn't sleep. They had lain in bed for hours, listening.... Then one of the children said, "Let us all go down and touch the tree and make a wish before we go to sleep." So very quietly ... they took their clothes under the covers and dressed themselves. They put on their sweaters and slippers and socks and bathrobes. In the big quiet house where the people were sleeping, the children got out of their beds. Then into the upstairs hall they went—quietly, almost without breathing ... past the door where Mother and Father were sleeping. So quietly through the hall. No sound until the top stair creaked. Then they all stood terribly still and listened. No sound but their own thumping hearts.

"ON CHRISTMAS EVE," MARGARET WISE BROWN

A CHILD'S VIEW *of St. Nicholas, the original Santa Claus, is the work of a five-year-old Dutch girl. He wears a bishop's robes.*

# THE
# WONDER
# OF JESUS'
# BIRTHDAY

TOTALLY ABSORBED *in his bag of Christmas candies, a German boy sits under a European-style tree adorned with real candles.*

ALTHOUGH all the world joyously celebrates Christmas, no one knows whether Jesus as a boy ever had a birthday party. Except for kings and important people who lived in palaces, the Jews of His time held no special celebrations for their birthdays, although they kept track of their years. But if certain pious legends are to be believed, Jesus had an enchanted childhood nevertheless, with or without birthday parties.

Even as a new baby, while still in the manger, these old stories go, He took pity on the tiniest camel in the whole caravan of the Magi. This diminutive dromedary reached Jesus' birthplace nearly exhausted from climbing up one side and sliding down the other of an endless succession of sand dunes. In reward the divine baby gave him eternal life, and even today, it is said, he gallops all over the Middle East on Christmas Eve bringing presents to boys and girls. Jesus, these stories say, did many other things. He made mud-pie birds one rainy day, and after His last pat, they flew away.

He rewarded the palm tree that bowed down to give its fruit to His holy mother by having an angel take a cutting from the tree and plant it in paradise.

It can be guessed that He lived in a little house aromatic with the sweet smell of new wood from His father's carpentry shop. It is certain that He had kind and gentle parents who loved Him very much, and it is not hard to imagine that His mother, at least, noted His birthday anniversaries in her heart.

In every story of Jesus' boyhood, there is something of the wonder that every child feels at Christmas. Of all the people in the house, the delights of Christmas belong first to the children. For them Christmas is more wonderful (and takes longer to come) than for anyone else. This is their season of glory. Excitement begins with the first rehearsals of the school play. Mothers are busy sewing tunics for shepherds and wings for angels. Suddenly downtown is all dressed up in lights, and Christmas carols are heard in the streets. School tingles with the excitement of decorating classrooms and wrapping presents (with a 50-cent limit on their cost) for the Christmas party grab bag.

Vacation comes at last. At home Christmas is even more exciting; everyone is astir with plots and plans. There are trips to see Santa and tours of inspection of the brightly decorated stores in the big city. There are lists to be made and sent to Santa or whispered into receptive ears if the right presents are to come.

In fact, there are no end of things to do at Christmas. It is a time for wresting control of the kitchen for at least a little while and baking cookies, or taking over the living room for a night and giving a play, or commandeering the whole house and holding a party. Christmas is the time to play games, make collages, plan decorations. It is also the time to spill out of the house to see the fireworks displays in the South, or go on nighttime skating parties and hay rides under the wintry stars in the North. And amid all these joys, there are agonizing decisions to make about presents.

There is a curious thing about presents. Everyone knows they come from the little camel galloping about the Middle East, or from *Los Sabios* (the Wise Men) in Latin America, or *Christkindl* (Christ child) in Germany, or Père Noël (Father Christmas) in France, or Santa Claus in America. And yet, by the time you are seven you also know that presents come from the love a family has for one another. And by that time, you are old enough to be a kind of Santa Claus yourself, bringing home the presents you have made in school, going shopping on your own and finding a hiding place in the grandfather's clock, under the cellar stairs or in the laundry hamper to keep them safe until Christmas.

Then at last it is time to take these treasures to your own room, and with barricaded door and a lavish supply of colored paper, ribbons, scissors and tape, to begin the absorbing job of wrapping them. It takes patience and more fingers than most children have to tie up the pomander ball, made of an orange stuck full of cloves, or the cuff-links box for Daddy—an old coffee can sprayed with gilt and encrusted with crushed marbles. But the thrill of placing your own gifts under the tree, even if they are a bit lumpy, makes it all worth while.

CRITICAL MOMENTS EVERY CHRISTMAS *come with the present-wrapping (above). The seals come unstuck and the scissors vanish (but you can find them) and you run out of tags, but the main trouble is that presents come in funny shapes, and some have no shape at all. You're lucky if you have an older sister to help tie bows—but who's going to help you wrap her gift?*

# TIME TO GIVE A PLAY

Plays about the Three Wise Men have been put on since the time of Robin Hood and before—a long, long time ago. At first they were performed only in churches, as part of the services at Christmastime. In one version, three men dressed like kings would come down different aisles, point to a big star hanging from the ceiling and present their gifts at the altar. Herod, the wicked king, would suddenly appear to try to make them tell him where Jesus was sleeping. In order to escape Herod, the Wise Men would duck down a side aisle. In later versions of these old plays, Herod became meaner and meaner, until finally he was given a sword which he would use to slash the air as he shouted his nasty threats to the Wise Men.

These plays eventually became great spectacles. In one Italian city, when the big day arrived, the Three Wise Men would march through the streets, preceded by trumpets and horns and followed by "apes, baboons, and diverse kinds of animals."

The play at the right may not have any baboons, but it does have diverse other animals. You and your friends can perform the parts yourselves, or you can make puppets and give a puppet show. If you don't have time to memorize the words, you can study them, then sit down with your family and read the parts aloud. If the idea of a puppet show sounds interesting, you will find at the end of the play instructions on how to make a theater and puppets as well as ideas for scenery and costumes for this particular play.

# THE JOURNEY OF THE THREE KINGS

## Condensed and Adapted from the Play by Henri Ghéon

*( Night, Backdrop of desert and starry sky. The Three Kings appear, one in the middle, the others at the right and left, followed by camel, elephant and other animals. A moment's music.)*

THE THREE MAGI: The Magi from the East are we;
   The Three Wise Kings you always see
   When Christmas turns to Epiphany!
   Look at our elephants, clumpety-clump!
   Look at our camels, humpety-hump!
   Look at our turbans, wrappety-wrap;
   Hark how our shoes go tappety-tap!
   Oh silver shoes, and silken dress—
   And in our eyes, what happiness!
FIRST MAGUS: I am the King of Chaldea.
SECOND MAGUS: I am the King of Arabia.
THIRD MAGUS: I am the King of Ethiopia.
THE THREE MAGI *(in turn)*: Balthazar! —Melchior!—And Caspar!
BALTHAZAR: Every night, when the sky is fine, we pull our telescopes out of their covers—
MELCHIOR: And we turn them on the sky at night, to watch the movements of the stars.
CASPAR: For all knowledge lives in the heavens.

*(They look toward the sky. Pause.)*

BALTHAZAR: Nothing new?
MELCHIOR: Nothing new. The sky doesn't change as quick as all that. Still it is so lovely that one never gets tired of it. And yet . . . you remember the prophecy? "There

shall rise up a Star out of Jacob; a King shall arise from the midst of Israel." The King of the Jews! We shall see God! He will send us His star.
BALTHAZAR: If we have faith enough in Him.
MELCHIOR: If we pray hard to Him.
CASPAR: If that is so, let us pray—pray hard! We will wait, prostrate on the ground, till He does answer.

*(They lie down, faces to the ground. A slight pause, then, an Angel enters. She has a wand in her hand, long and flexible like a fishing rod, with a great star at its end.)*

ANGEL: I am the shepherd of the stars. I urge them forward with my wand, like a flock of white sheep, day and night. When evening comes, their spiritual light falls on the poor, the wanderer, on sailors who have no beacon, on children with no parents, on all who are seeking for their path. *(Pause.)* God said to me: "Join your two hands, and then open them wide, my child. I am going to place between them the loveliest star of all. Let the star loose, if you will, and urge it forward with your wand. They who watch the sky shall see it, and love it, and, maybe, follow it. They shall see it come to rest upon the stable where My Son is born." *(She moves slowly forward with the star at the end of her wand.)*
CASPAR *(raising his head)*: Oh . . .
MELCHIOR and BALTHAZAR: What?
CASPAR: God has answered us. Look!
MELCHIOR: A new star! It looks as if it were calling us.
BALTHAZAR: Are we going off our heads, my lords? Are we becoming silly old men who look at the skies so long that we start to invent stars?

*(The Angel sets the star rocking.)*

CASPAR: No, no. We aren't dreaming. It's beckoning us to follow it. *(They fall on their faces, then get up.)* Forward! Let's just collect a few things—some food—some presents!

*(They move off behind the star, singing as before.)*

THE THREE MAGI: The Magi from the
    East are we;
    The Three Wise Kings you always
      see
    When Christmas turns to Epiph-
      any!
    Look at our elephants, clumpety-
      clump!
    Look at our camels, humpety-
      hump!
    Look at our turbans, wrappety-
      wrap;
    Hark how our shoes go tappety-
      tap!
    Oh silver shoes and silken dress!
    And in our eyes, what happiness!
    *(They leave.)*

*(Having gone out on one side, they return on the other side, behind the Angel. They are escorted by elephants, camels and zebras. They pass and repass several times. Gradually their speed slackens, they falter, they become very tired. Then the Angel turns and says—)*

ANGEL *(to the Kings)*: Rest, now: go to sleep. Jerusalem is quite near. My star will wait for you, never fear. *(The Kings look at one another.)*

THE THREE MAGI *(to the star)*: Have we got there? *(The star indicates "No" by swinging back and forth.)* Not yet?

CASPAR: Should we go to sleep a little so as to be fresh when we present ourselves to the great King? *(The star bobs up and down "Yes.")* Thank you! *(To the elephant and the camel behind them.)* Lie down, good creatures! *(The beasts obey. The Magi lie down and go to sleep. The Angel goes quietly away.)*

*(After a while a night watchman comes in carrying a lantern. He collides with the Kings and steps back, astonished.)*

NIGHT WATCHMAN: Now then, what's all this? Now it's gypsies! or fortune-tellers? vagabonds? Get up! Get up! You can't sleep here. You have to sleep at home. And if you haven't got a home, you must sleep at the police station.

THE THREE MAGI *(waking up and rubbing their eyes)*: What's the mat-

ter?—Time to start again?—The star's gone away. . . .

NIGHT WATCHMAN: Up with you. *(They get up.)* Coo! You've got fine clothes. Where did you steal all that? *(The elephant and camel wake up.)* An elephant? a dromedary? *(Looking off.)* Zebras—horses—llamas—parrots—monkeys—ostriches! What a procession! But it's the Queen of Saba all over again. Who are you? What have you come for?

CASPAR: We have come to see the King of the Jews and to worship him. Is this the right place?

NIGHT WATCHMAN: This is right, my lords. The king's called Herod. There's nothing he'd like better than to be worshiped, yes sirs.

CASPAR: Can we be taken to him?

NIGHT WATCHMAN: It's very late. But when he knows that you want to worship him, with elephants and ostriches and camels—he'll jump out of bed if he's in it, yes sirs!

CASPAR: The star has not deceived us, you see, my lords. *(They follow the Watchman. Curtain.)*

*(The curtain rises, showing a backdrop of*

*The Three Kings, bearing gifts, their heads lifted to see the star which is guiding them to Bethlehem, lead the procession across the desert.*

*Kneeling at the manger, the Three Kings are allowed to kiss the baby Mary presents to them.*

*Herod's palace. Enter Herod, wearing his royal cloak.)*

HEROD: Three eastern kings? Very second-rate kings. Come to worship me? Not so impossible. There are no gods left. After all, people have to worship *someone*. *(Enter Kings one by one who give their names and bow.)* Your Majesties are very welcome. We wait your homage. *(The Magi do not stir. Herod repeats—)* We await their homage. *(Silence again. Herod shouts—)* We await their homage!

CASPAR *(timidly and whispering):* We heard quite well, sir; but isn't there some mistake? What is the name of this king? There must be two. Forgive us. We must go and look for the other one. *(They bow and are about to retire, but Herod speaks.)*

HEROD: What are you whispering about? What is the matter?

BALTHAZAR: If his Majesty King Herod will forgive us, we—er—

HEROD: Well?

MELCHIOR: His personal appearance does not quite correspond, perhaps. . .

CASPAR: With the information we received. There!

BALTHAZAR: The King of the Jews that we came to worship—

MELCHIOR: Whose star we followed—

CASPAR: Is only just born. He hasn't a beard, Sire . . . He's still quite a small baby. Could you perhaps tell us where to find Him? *(Herod scowls. After a long silence he draws closer.)*

HEROD: Forgive me, my lords. Quite so. There is a mistake. I am indeed delighted beyond words to know that my successor, who is to take my place—a long time hence . . . when I am old and good for nothing . . . has at last appeared in this world. Bring me the chief priests!

*( The chief priests, in long robes with fringes, come pompously in.)*

HEROD: Reverend Sirs, can you tell me where the King of the Jews is to be born? I mean the one that your prophets foretold.

CHIEF PRIESTS: Yes, Your Majesty. At Bethlehem of Juda. *(They intone):* "And thou, Bethlehem, land of Juda, thou art not the least among the chief cities of Juda, for from thee shall come forth the prince who shall rule Israel, My people."

THE THREE MAGI: Bethlehem? Bethlehem?

HEROD: Your Majesties heard? Kindly go ahead of me to Bethlehem.

To make sure, I shall entreat you to come back this way and call at our palace to inform me of the result of your inquiries.

BALTHAZAR *(going out):* Certainly, Sire. But does no one know this king?

MELCHIOR: How shall we find his house?

CASPAR *(pointing to the sky):* Hush! The star!

HEROD *(watching them):* What are you looking at in the sky, my lords?

THE THREE MAGI: Nothing . . . nothing . . .

CASPAR: Just to see if it is likely to be fine, Your Majesty. *(They go out.)*

HEROD *(to the Chief Priests):* Please make your due arrangements. Thank you. *(They go out. Herod stamps, and shouts—)* No, no, no, no! The King of the Jews? *I'm* that. I'm that! *I'm* the King of the Jews. *(Shouting after the priests.)* See that they keep an eye on those three fellows. *(Curtain.)*

*(Backdrop of desert and stars. The Three Kings once more on their travels, the Angel going in front with the Star on her wand.)*

CASPAR: As for me, I don't trust that old king.

ANGEL *(softly):* He is lying. He wants to do the Child a hurt.

MELCHIOR: No; he can't be a wicked man. He wants to come and worship Him.

ANGEL: So he says.

MELCHIOR: It's certainly very odd.

CASPAR: My lords, you distress me. Why try to understand, when all you've got to do is to look? The star is before us; it guides us. What more do you want? *(He pauses.)* Ah! *(The Angel has halted at one side.)*

MELCHIOR: What's the matter?

CASPAR: Our star has stopped. It's here! This is the royal palace . . . *(looking off-stage).*

MELCHIOR: A palace? You're dreaming. This cave?

BALTHAZAR: This old hole? The little King here? In this stable?

MELCHIOR *(sarcastically):* On the straw, perhaps?

BALTHAZAR: In the animals' manger?

THE OX (from off-stage): Moo! Moo!

THE ASS (from off-stage): Hee-haw! Hee-haw!

CASPAR: When you spoke, you didn't guess how right you were. It's a loving company for the little King of Peace. (Curtain.)

(Backdrop of cave. The Divine Child lies in the manger, the two animals beside Him, Mary and Joseph opposite one another.)

CASPAR: Between ox and ass!

ANGEL: Patience; humility!

THE THREE MAGI: How lovely the Child is! (They bow.)

ANGEL: Shall I tell your followers to come?

CASPAR: Keep them at a distance, so as not to draw a crowd. But let the gold, frankincense and myrrh be brought, and let the elephant and the camel be informed that they must, in the name of all animals, come and salute the Ox and the Ass.

JOSEPH (to Mary): Who are they?

MARY: Kings.

JOSEPH: We have nothing to offer them.

MARY: Nothing? But—my Baby?

JOSEPH: I mean nothing to eat or drink.

MARY: One doesn't feel how hungry one is—here.

(Kings go off-stage and come back with gifts. They lift their heads and see the elephant and the camel coming in.)

CASPAR: Here is the elephant. Elephant, say "good-morning" to the Ox.

BALTHAZAR: Here is the camel. Say "how do you do" to the Ass. (The animals kiss one another.)

CASPAR (to Mary and Joseph): Here we are in the presence of the little King, who has nothing on but these thin swaddling clothes, and we are quite ashamed to be so finely dressed. So we make over to Him our crowns and our turbans ... (they take them off) our mantles and our robes. (Unpinning robes.) With nothing left now but our underdress, we look like poor people. And unluckily there's nothing much inside us without our gorgeous array. But as for Him, dear little fellow, He needs but to be—just as He is, in order to shine! Oh, the lovely little King! May He teach us to shine, like Him, inside our souls.

MELCHIOR: And now, here is Gold, from Arabia.

BALTHAZAR: Here is Incense, from Chaldea.

CASPAR: Here is the Myrrh of Ethiopia. (They put their gifts down.)

BALTHAZAR: Before we leave, could we kiss the Baby?

MARY: Yes, I give Him to you. (Kings lean over the manger and kiss the Child.)

BALTHAZAR (as he rises, deeply moved): I shall never forget this moment. Now we must take the news back to King Herod.

VOICE OF THE ANGEL (from off-stage): No.

BALTHAZAR (to Caspar): Why not? You said No ...

CASPAR: I never spoke.

BALTHAZAR: Well, I repeat; we must take the news back to King Herod.

ANGEL (very loud): No, no!

MELCHIOR: I heard it this time.

CASPAR: Someone said No.

BALTHAZAR: But who?

CASPAR: Someone shrewder than us ...

ANGEL: And who is anxious for the Child.

BALTHAZAR: But what is she anxious about?

CASPAR: If you were the king of the Jews and someone came to tell you that another king of the Jews, the real one, had just been born, so as to take your place, would you be very pleased?

BALTHAZAR: Obviously not.

CASPAR: Well, then, let's be on our guard and not go back by Herod. We will go home by a different way round, in our rough tunics, like peasants. (They go out leaving animals behind. Curtain.)

(Backdrop of desert and stars. Enter the Night Watchman, apparently looking for someone. Enter Kings opposite. He calls to them.)

NIGHT WATCHMAN: Hi! You there! Have you seen the three kings? With turbans and crowns? Their caravan is awaiting them.

MELCHIOR, then BALTHAZAR: Kings?

CASPAR: Kings? No; we haven't seen any kings, my friend. We are quite poor people.

NIGHT WATCHMAN: Well, good-night. (As he turns away.) Where can they have gone? (Exit. When he is gone, the Kings burst out laughing.)

BALTHAZAR: Stupid man. He thinks you recognize a king just by his clothes.

MELCHIOR: Oh; they all think that. Be honest; didn't we think so ourselves?

CASPAR: Yes; we didn't know.

BALTHAZAR: If that is so, we're well disguised. (They go out arm-in-arm, singing—)
The Magi from the East are we,
But not like those you always see
When Christmas turns to Epiphany!
Never an elephant, clumpety-clump;
Never a camel, all humpety-hump!
Not even a turban, wrappety-wrap;
Nor any more shoes that go tappety-tap!
No silver shoes, no silken dress—
With nothing left but happiness!

*CURTAIN*

The Kings start the long trip home.

Desert can be the deep blue of night.

Herod's palace needs a bright color.

Manger scene may be done in green.

For scene changes, draw the curtains shut and tape the next backdrop (shown at right) to the panel door behind the stage. Now that you've set the scene, open the curtain and on with the show.

# BACKSTAGE WITH PUPPETS

A puppet show is easily staged. The main thing you need is something big enough to hide behind (perhaps by crouching), yet low enough so you can reach above it comfortably with the puppets on your hands. You can simply hang a sheet across the lower half of a doorway, or turn a large table on its side, or hide behind a low desk or dresser. A more professional-looking stage is made from a very large box—perhaps a cardboard wardrobe or a refrigerator carton. A box gives you not only a place to hide but a back wall for backdrops. Certain stores will sell you these boxes for a small sum, and they can be kept and made into permanent stages for later puppet shows.

For the stage, cut a rectangular opening in the upper half of the face of the box. Decorate the box in any way that you think will make it look more like a theater. Baste curtains on a string and tack them into place above the stage. To light the set, cut out a square in the top of the box and place the box under a light —a very tall floor lamp or overhead light. In order to get in and out of the box, you will have to slit open three sides of the back of the box, leaving one long side attached. Now the back of the box can be opened like a door that is hinged on one side. Cut off the lower part of this back door entirely, right up to where the stage begins. All you have left is a back for the stage.

You will need to make five sock puppets: Herod, the Three Kings, and the Night Watchman. Use solid-color socks that have ribbed cuffs. Stuff some cotton loosely into sock toe. Tape a cylinder of cardboard around the whole length of your index finger, then push the cylinder well up into cotton and pack more cotton around it, until you have a round head about as big as a tennis ball. The lower end of the cylinder

slit hands

pleat skirt

wand

slit

draw face

popsicle stick

*Draw outline of angel on blue paper, cut out arms, wings and slits as shown above. Wand is strip of paper 1" wide. Fringe by making four snips, fold paper lengthwise four times and tape. Thread wand first through slits in star, then angel. Bend fringes back to make star's rays.*

stuff toe

cardboard cylinder

armholes

cut off cuff

fringed beard

*Kings' outer robes should be quite rich, like velvet or brocade or silk. You can embroider them further with sequins, gold or pearl buttons, and bits of inked cotton to represent ermine. Pin around necks of puppets for easy removal. Shoes hang by threads sewn to bottom of socks.*

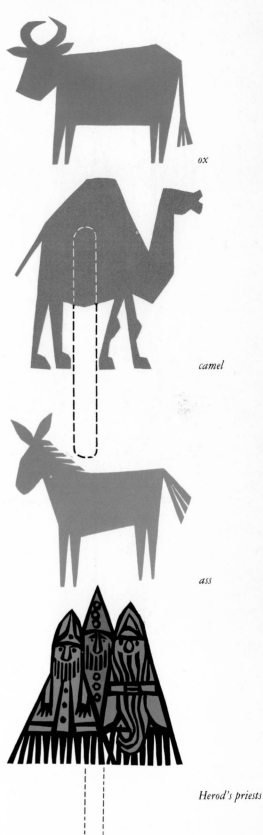

ox

camel

ass

Herod's priests

*Draw the animals and high priests on thin cardboard. Cut out and paint with poster paints. Glue the different shapes to popsicle sticks. The three high priests are cut from one piece of cardboard and move as a group.*

is the neck. Tie string tightly around the neck, outside the sock. For armholes, cut two small holes on opposite sides of the sock below the neck. For costumes, fold a piece of handkerchief-size cloth double, cut a penny-size hole in the center of fold for neck. Cut out simple dress shape with sleeves and baste sleeves. Thread the bottom of the sock through neck hole; tape or paste the costume to the neck. Outline eyes, noses and mouths in black or paste colored shapes on faces instead. Herod's costume should be kingly (a scrap of fancy cloth), the Night Watchman's and the Kings' very plain. The Kings'

removable cloaks should be as rich as you can find or make, but they are simply pieces of cloth pinned around Kings' necks. Turbans are three-cornered bits of cloth knotted at forehead. Cutout crowns go on top. Snip shoes for each King from silver paper or foil. They will dance freely if threaded on long thread sewn to bottom of socks.

Herod at least must have a beard. Beards and hair are made by cutting off ribbed cuffs of the socks. Fringe each cuff and slide it around head, under chin. The pictures on this page suggest how to make cutouts for the other characters in the play.

87

## NEW USES
## FOR
## THE COLORS OF
## CHRISTMAS

Color is one of the best parts of Christmas; no other season is so rich in reds, greens, blues, golds and silvers. A tremendous amount of color comes in the form of bright wrapping paper and splendid big ribbons and bows that deserve to be used more than once. Perhaps late Christmas afternoon you can tidy up the living room by gathering all the wrappings lying about and then use them to make collages. Collages are pasted-up pictures—such as the three on these pages—of Christmas scenes, or trains, or ships, or little girls dancing under the tree, or anything. All that is needed is cardboard, scissors, big batches of colored paper and ribbons, some paste or rubber cement and a little elbow room.

First, the cardboard—say the top of a Christmas box—is selected to make a back for the picture, and then your shears begin to cut the figures you have thought out in the colors and papers and ribbons that you like the best. These you paste in place on the cardboard, together with anything else you think fit—cotton, broom straws, pipe cleaners, even macaroni and noodles—until the picture you had in mind is done.

A VISIT FROM ST. NICK *naturally begins with a cutout fireplace and a glittery green tree. Packages are easy to paste up, and bits of cotton are a great help with Santa's beard, belt and cap.*

THE NATIVITY SCENE *has a stable outlined in ribbons. The cow and the donkey are not so hard to cut out as one might think. Plain grocery store paper is a good idea for the baby and the faces.*

THE THREE WISE MEN, *bearing gifts, are marching over a glistening green landscape past a ribbon palm tree. The camels were cut from yellow shelf paper that was stolen from the kitchen.*

**MUSIC AND SCRAMBLES**

*Musical Chairs is scrambling and laughter. There is one less chair than there are children. The children march around the chairs, and when the music stops, each runs for a chair. One child and one chair are out each round until two compete for the last chair.*

# NINE NOISY GAMES FOR INDOOR FUN

The fun and excitement of games at Christmas is second best only to presents. Games stir things up, get everyone tense and a-shiver to win and then let laughter loose. Sometimes at Christmas, grownups can be lured into joining, and this increases the fun, for it is always nice to bring Daddy to bay. And best of all, the rules against yelling indoors and pounding up and down stairs are off. Streams of noisy children can pursue one another all through the house and no one scolds or says a word.

The trick of making a Christmas party successful is planning in advance so that things move along at a galloping pace. Grownups are great helps with parties, but children will want to plan the most exciting parts themselves. To help in the planning, here are nine ever-popular games, illustrated by charming figurines from *Lady Tabitha and Us*, a favorite holiday book early in this century.

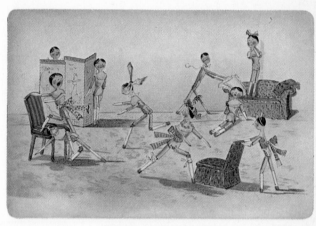

**DIZZINESS AND GUESSES**

*Traditional with Christmas is the merry game of Blindman's Buff. A player is blindfolded, turned around and sent reeling to catch someone. Players can poke and shout to confuse him. If he can name his catch, the one caught becomes next to be blindfolded.*

**NUTS AND WRESTLING**

*Here We Go Gathering Nuts in May is too delightful to be out of season at Christmas. Singing the old song (page 99), one team picks a "nut," the other a "puller," who Indian-wrestle. The loser changes sides and the game goes on until all are on one side.*

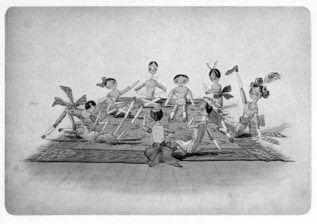

**GIGGLES AND SECRETS**

*To Hunt the Slipper the children sit in a circle. "It" tosses in a slipper singing, "Cobbler, cobbler mend my shoe. Have it done by half past two." While the giggling players secretly pass the slipper to one another, "it" runs about outside trying to guess who has it.*

**HIDINGS AND RUNNINGS**

*Hide and Seek starts with "it" counting to 100 while everyone hides. Then "it" calls, "A bushel of wheat, a bushel of clover, all not hid can't hide over," and comes looking. When he finds someone, there is a race to base and if "it" wins, the other is "it."*

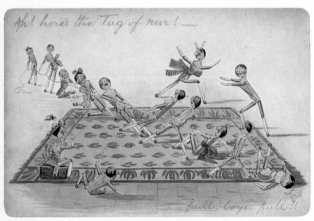

**SQUEALS AND PULLINGS**

*Tug of War, certain to set up squeals of fury, needs pulling space. A rope with a handkerchief tied to its middle is so laid that the handkerchief is halfway between two lines on the ground. Each team pulls against the other to get the handkerchief over its line.*

**HANKIES AND MUSH POTS**

*In Drop the Handkerchief "it" drops a handkerchief behind one of the children in a circle who must pick it up and pursue him. If the dropper is caught he must go to the mush pot, or center. He can escape by grabbing a handkerchief dropped behind another.*

**FRUITS AND CAPTIVES**

*Under an arch formed by two players the rest march singing "Oranges and Lemons" (page 99). The arch falls and one by one traps the players who secretly choose apples or pears—a blind choice. The resulting teams, often uneven, then hold a tug of war.*

**GUESSING AND ACTING**

*In Dumb Crambo, a variety of Charades, the audience selects a word, perhaps "bell," and tells the actors it rhymes with "sell." First guessing wrong, the actors yell, while the audience groans. Then guessing right, the actors toll a bell and the audience cheers.*

# HOW
# MANY GAMES
# ARE HERE?

The most exciting thing that could possibly happen to a child on a magical Christmas would be throwing open a window and looking down on the happy and busy world that is shown in the picture at right. Here is a townful of children—not one grownup among all the dozens and dozens of youngsters larking about in the streets and yard, at the windows, on the steps and porches, or among the swimmers splashing in the river. It is summer, which is quite a Christmas miracle all by itself, and everyone is romping together at games or playing with toys. The picture is so full of merriment and fun that you can almost hear the children's happy shouts.

All this happened 400 years ago when Pieter Bruegel, a jovial artist who lived in what is now Belgium, and who liked to play merry tricks on his friends, painted the picture. Perhaps he painted the scene because it was a jolly thing to see, or perhaps he wanted to show people how to play all the games children played when he was a boy. Whichever, the amazing thing is that almost all of these games are still being played at parties and in schoolyards. Some of them, like leapfrog and blindman's buff pop out of the picture at you and you notice them right off. But it takes careful looking to spot, amid all the delightful doings taking place in all parts of the picture, many others, such as shout into a barrel or beat the kettle.

No one knows how many games are pictured here. A diagram with a list of 71 is printed on page 94. But it is possible that someone who knows many games might pore over every inch of the picture and find a 72nd.

92

# Key to the Bruegel Game Puzzle

*This diagram indicates the 71 games that have been counted (perhaps there are even more) in the Pieter Bruegel painting shown on pages 92-93. Almost every game in 16th Century painting is still played today in exactly the way Bruegel pictured it or only slightly altered.*

1 JACKS
2 DOLLS
3 RATTLE
4 THREE LITTLE MILLS—an animated toy
5 BLOWING BUBBLES
6 PLAYING WITH A PET BIRD
7 MAKE-BELIEVE CHRISTENING
8 CARRY MY LADY TO LONDON
9 HOBBYHORSE
10 FIFE AND DRUM
11 MUD PIE
12 HOOPS
13 SHOUTING INTO A BARREL
14 RIDING A BARREL
15 BLOWING UP A BALLOON—really a pig's bladder
16 JOHNNY ON THE PONY
17 MAKE-BELIEVE STORE
18 MUMBLETY-PEG
19 BUILDING BLOCKS—really bricks
20 BOUNCE THE BABY
21 LEAPFROG
22 DUEL ON HORSEBACK OR TUG OF WAR
23 ODD OR EVEN OR GUESS WHICH HAND?
24 RUNNING THE GANTLET
25 BLINDMAN'S BUFF
26 ROLLING STONE

OR WAGON WHEEL
27 SOMERSAULT
28 HEADSTAND
29 POPGUN OR PEASHOOTER
30 MASK
31 SWING
32 SAND PILE
33 FENCE-CLIMBING
34 KING OF THE HILL
35 TILTING OR TOURNAMENT WITH WINDMILLS
36 RIDING A FENCE
37 MAKE-BELIEVE WEDDING PROCESSION
38 BEAT THE KETTLE —blindfolded boy tries to hit kettle
39 STILTS
40 HAT-TOSSING
41 PULLING HAIR
42 KILLING FLIES
43 CATCH THE WOODEN FISH
44 CASTLES—knocking over "castles" made of marbles
45 THROWING KNUCKLEBONES—similar to ninepins
46 TIP-CAT
47 MARBLES
48 DEVIL ON THE CHAIN—trying to escape "devil" who is attached

by length of chain to player
49 CLIMBING CELLAR DOOR
50 WRESTLING
51 CRACK THE WHIP
52 MAKE-BELIEVE PARADE
53 HANDSPAN OR BANGER—tossing coins against wall
54 PLAYING GATEKEEPER
55 PLAYING AT ASKING FOR GIRL'S HAND IN MARRIAGE
56 RIDING ON SHOULDERS
57 FOLLOW THE LEADER
58 PUSH OFF THE BENCH
59 BAYARD—four brothers on a horse
60 BUILDING A BONFIRE
61 SWINGING ON HITCHING RAIL
62 BROOM BALANCING
63 PIGGYBACK
64 WHIPPING TOPS
65 ST. NICHOLAS' BASKETS—good children get shoes; bad ones get switches
66 FLYING A RIBBON
67 BOWLING
68 WHO AM I GOING TO CHOOSE?
69 TURN YOURSELF AROUND
70 TREE-CLIMBING
71 SWIMMING (with pig's bladder water wings)

# The Tree That Didn't Get Trimmed

*In the story below, the American novelist, poet and playwright, Christopher Morley (1890-1957) tells youthful readers about a fir sapling that found a happy career despite the frustration of a lifelong ambition to be a Christmas tree.*

If you walk through a grove of balsam trees you will notice that the young trees are silent; they are listening. But the old tall ones—especially the firs—are whispering. They are telling the story of The Tree That Didn't Get Trimmed. It sounds like a painful story, and the murmur of the old trees as they tell it is rather solemn; but it is an encouraging story for young saplings to hear . . .

The tree in this story should never have been cut. He wouldn't have been, but it was getting dark in the Vermont woods, and the man with the ax said to himself, "Just one more." Cutting young trees with a sharp, beautifully balanced ax is fascinating; you go on and on; there's a sort of cruel pleasure in it. The blade goes through the soft wood with one whistling stroke and the boughs sink down with a soft swish.

He was a fine, well-grown youngster, but too tall for his age; his branches were rather scraggly. If he'd been left there he would have been an unusually big tree some day; but now he was in the awkward age and didn't have the tapering shape and the thick, even foliage that people like on Christmas trees. Worse still, instead of running up to a straight, clean spire, his top was a bit lop-sided, with a fork in it.

But he didn't know this as he stood with many others, leaning against the side wall of the green-grocer's shop. In those cold December days he was very happy, thinking of the pleasures to come. He had heard of the delights of Christmas Eve: the stealthy setting-up of the tree, the tinsel balls and coloured toys and stars, the peppermint canes and birds with spun-glass tails. Even that old anxiety of Christmas trees—burning candles—did not worry him, for he had been told that nowadays people use strings of tiny electric bulbs which cannot set one on fire. So he looked forward to the festival with a confident heart.

"I shall be very grand," he said. "I hope there will be children to admire me. It must be a great moment when the children hang their stockings on you!" He even felt sorry for the first trees that were chosen and taken away. It would be best, he considered, not to be bought until Christmas Eve. Then, in the shining darkness someone would pick him out, put him carefully along the running board of a car, and away they would go. The tire-chains would clack and jingle merrily on the snowy road. He imagined a big house with a fire glowing on a hearth; the hushed rustle of wrapping paper and parcels being unpacked. Someone would say, "Oh, what a beautiful tree!" How erect and stiff he would brace himself in his iron tripod stand.

But day after day went by, one by one the other trees were taken, and he began to grow troubled. For everyone who looked at him seemed to have an unkind word. "Too tall," said one lady. "No, this one wouldn't do, the branches are too skimpy," said another. "If I chop off the top," said the green-grocer, "it wouldn't be so bad?" The tree shuddered . . . Then he was shown to a lady who wanted a tree very cheap. "You can have this one for a dollar," said the grocer. This was only one third of what the grocer had asked for him at first, but even so the lady refused him . . .

Now it was Christmas Eve. It was a foggy evening with a drizzling rain; the alley alongside the store was thick with trampled slush. As he lay there among broken boxes and fallen scraps of holly strange thoughts came to him. In the still northern forest already his wounded stump was buried in forgetful snow. He remembered the wintry sparkle of the woods, the big trees with crusts and clumps of silver on their broad boughs, the keen singing of the lonely wind. He remembered the strong, warm feeling of his roots reaching down into the safe earth. That is a good feeling; it means to a tree just what it means to you to stretch your toes down toward the bottom of a well-tucked bed. And he had given up all this to lie here, disdained and forgotten, in a littered alley. The splash of feet, the chime of bells, the cry of cars went past him. He trembled a little with self-pity and vexation. "No toys and stockings for me," he thought sadly, and shed some of his needles.

Late that night, after all the shopping was over, the grocer came out to clear away what was left. The boxes, the broken wreaths, the empty barrels, and our tree with one or two others that hadn't been sold, all were thrown through the side door into the cellar. The door was locked and he lay there in the dark. One of his branches, doubled under him in the fall, ached so he thought it must be broken. "So this is Christmas," he said to himself.

All that day it was very still in the cellar. There was an occasional creak as one of the bruised trees tried to stretch itself. Feet went along the pavement overhead, and there was a booming of church bells, but everything had a slow, disappointed sound. Christmas is always a little sad, after such busy preparations. The unwanted trees lay on the stone floor, watching the furnace light flicker on a hatchet that had been left there.

The day after Christmas a man came in who wanted some green boughs. . . . The grocer took the hatchet, and seized the trees without ceremony. They were too disheartened to care. Chop, chop, chop, went the blade, and the sweet-smelling branches were carried away. The naked trunks were thrown into a corner.

And now our tree, what was left of him, had plenty of time to think. He no longer could feel anything, for trees feel with their branches, but they think with their trunks. What did he think about as he grew dry and stiff? He thought that it had been silly of him to imagine such a fine, gay career for himself, and he was sorry for other young trees, still growing in the fresh hilly country, who were enjoying the same fantastic dreams.

Now perhaps you don't know what happens to the trunks of left-over Christmas trees. You could never guess. Farmers come in from the suburbs and buy them at five cents each for bean-poles and grape arbours. So perhaps (here begins the encouraging part of this story) they are really happier, in the end, than the trees that get trimmed for Santa Claus. They go back into the fresh, moist earth of spring, and when the sun grows hot the quick tendrils of the vines climb up them and presently they are decorated with the red blossoms of the bean or the little blue globes of the grape, just as pretty as any Christmas trinkets.

So one day the naked, dusty fir-poles were taken out of the cellar, and thrown into a truck with many others, and made a rattling journey out into the land. The farmer unloaded them in his yard and was stacking them up by the barn when his wife came out to watch him.

"There!" she said. "That's just what I want, a nice long pole with a fork in it. Jim, put that one over there to hold up the clothesline." It was the first time that anyone had praised our tree, and his dried-up heart swelled with a tingle of forgotten sap. They put him near one end of the clothesline, with his stump close to a flower bed. The fork that

had been despised for a Christmas star was just the thing to hold up a clothesline. It was washday, and soon the farmer's wife began bringing out wet garments to swing and freshen in the clean, bright air. And the very first thing that hung near the top of the Christmas pole was a cluster of children's stockings.

That isn't quite the end of the story, as the old fir trees whisper it in the breeze. The Tree That Didn't Get Trimmed was so cheerful watching the stockings, and other gay little clothes that plumped out in the wind just as though waiting to be spanked, that he didn't notice what was going on—or going up—below him. A vine had caught hold of his trunk and was steadily twisting upward. And one morning when the farmer's wife came out intending to shift him, she stopped and exclaimed. "Why, I mustn't move this pole," she said. "The morning glory has run right up it." So it had, and our bare pole was blue and crimson with colour . . .

# The Littlest Camel

*Christian children in southern Syria believe that a little camel, rewarded with immortality by the infant Jesus, brings all their presents on Christmas Eve. The legend behind this tradition is recounted here by Elizabeth Retivov.*

Not all the peoples of the Middle East have chosen the way of Mohammed the Prophet, as you very well know. There are some who obey the commands of the Prophet Moses. Still others follow the teachings of the Prophet Jesus.

The story of the littlest camel deeply concerns those boys and girls who celebrate the Birthday of Jesus, for this camel plays an important part in those celebrations. It is he, and he alone, who brings the children their gifts on the night before Christmas . . .

It happened that, quite by accident, the small camel was included in the caravan of the Three Wise Men. For, being the littlest camel of all, he was certainly not much help. In fact, it took all his energy just to keep up with the rest of the full-grown camels. Ignored by all, he dragged himself up sandy dunes and slid down rocky hills, stumbled, picked himself up again and hop-skipped after the Wise Men's caravan, so as not to be left behind and miss seeing the Child.

At last the caravan arrived at the town of Bethlehem and came to a small stable on the outskirts of the town. There, outside the stable, stood the Child Jesus. Man and beast knelt down before such a wonderful Child. But so great was the fatigue of the littlest camel that his legs simply buckled beneath him and he flopped to the ground. There he lay, moaning and groaning like a desert wind. The Child Jesus was so moved by the exhaustion and devotion of the small camel that he took pity on it and blessed it with immortality.

So it happens that each year, on the Anniversary of that night, the littlest camel repeats his journey . . . stopping off on the way to leave gifts outside the houses of Christian boys and girls.

# Christmas Island

*This lighthearted word play on the name of a minuscule island in the Indian Ocean was written by Katharine Lee Bates (1859-1929), American poet and educator and author of the lyrics of the famous hymn, "America the Beautiful."*

*Fringed with coral, floored with lava,*
*Three-score leagues to south of Java,*
*So is Christmas Island charted*
*By geographers blind-hearted,*
*—Just a dot, by their dull notion,*
*On the burning Indian Ocean;*
*Merely a refreshment station*
*For the birds in long migration;*
*Its pomegranates, custard-apples*
*That the dancing sunshine dapples,*
*Cocoanuts with milky hollows*
*Only feast wing-weary swallows*
*Or the tropic fowl there dwelling....*
*Don't believe a word they're telling!*
*Christmas Island, though it seem land,*
*Is a floating bit of dreamland*
*Gone adrift from childhood, planted*
*By the winds with seeds enchanted,*
*Seeds of candied plum and cherry:*
*Here the Christmas Saints make merry.*

*Even saints must have vacation;*
*So they chose from all creation*
*As a change from iceberg castles*
*Hung with snow in loops and tassels,*
*Christmas Island for a summer*
*Residence. The earliest comer*
*Is our own saint, none diviner,*
*Santa Claus. His ocean-liner*
*Is a sleigh that's scudding fast.*
*Mistletoe climbs up the mast,*
*And the sail so full of caper,*
*Is of tissue wrapping paper.*
*As he steers, he hums a carol;*
*But instead of fur apparel*
*Smudged with soot, he's spick and spandy*
*In white linen, dear old dandy.*
*With a Borealis sash on,*
*And a palm-leaf hat in fashion*
*Wreathed about with holly berry.*
*Welcome, Santa! Rest you merry!*

*Next, his chubby legs bestriding*
*Such a Yule-log, who comes riding*
*Overseas, the feast to dish up,*
*But—aha!—the boys' own bishop,*
*Good St. Nicholas! And listen!*
*Out of Denmark, old Jule-nissen,*
*Kindly goblin, bent rheumatic,*
*In the milk-bowl set up attic*
*For his Christmas cheer, comes bobbing*
*Through the waves. He'll be hob-nobbing*
*With Knecht Clobes, Dutchman true,*
*Sailing in a wooden shoe.*
*When the sunset gold enamels*
*All the sea, three cloudy camels*
*Bear the King with stately paces,*
*Taking islands for oases,*
*While a star-boat brings Kriss Kringle.*
*Singing Noël as they mingle,*
*Drinking toasts in sunshine sherry!*
*How the Christmas Saints make merry!*

*While a gray contralto pigeon*
*Coos that loving is religion,*
*How they laugh and how they rollick,*
*How they fill the isle with frolic.*
*Up the Christmas Trees they clamber,*
*Lighting candles rose and amber,*
*Till the sudden moonbeams glisten.*
*They all kneel but old Jule-nissen,*
*(Who, a heathen elf stiff-jointed,*
*Doffs his night-cap, red and pointed)*
*For within the moon's pale luster*
*They behold bright figures cluster;*

*Their adoring eyes look on a*
*Silver-throned serene Madonna,*
*With the Christ-Child, rosy sweeting,*
*Smiling to their loyal greeting.*
*Would that on this Holy Night*
*We might share such blissful sight,*
*—We might find a fairy ferry*
*To that isle where saints make merry!*

*So, a little Child, come down*
*And hear a child's tongue like Thy own;*
*Take me by the hand and walk,*
*And listen to my baby-talk.*
*To Thy Father show my prayer*
*(He will look, Thou art so fair),*
*And say: "O Father, I, Thy Son,*
*Bring the prayer of a little one."*
*And He will smile, that children's tongue*
*Has not changed since Thou wast young!*

# a child's prayer

*In these lines from a poem by Francis Thompson
(1859-1907), entitled "Little Jesus," a child
wonders about the childhood of the Savior.*

Ex ore infantium, Deus, et lactenium
  perfecisti laudem
*Little Jesus, wast Thou shy*
  *Once, and just so small as I?*
*And what did it feel like to be*
*Out of Heaven, and just like me?*
*Didst Thou sometimes think of there,*
*And ask where all the angels were?*
*I should think that I would cry*
*For my house all made of sky;*
*I would look about the air,*
*And wonder where my angels were;*
*And at waking 'twould distress me—*
*Not an angel there to dress me!*
*Hadst Thou ever any toys,*
*Like us little girls and boys?*
*And didst Thou play in Heaven with all*
*The angels that were not too tall,*
*With stars for marbles? Did the things*
*Play Can you see me? through their wings?*
*And did Thy Mother let Thee spoil*
*Thy robes, with playing on our soil?*
*How nice to have them always new*
*In Heaven, because 'twas quite clean blue! . . .*
*Thou canst not have forgotten all*
*That it feels like to be small:*
*And Thou know'st I cannot pray*
*To Thee in my father's way—*
*When Thou wast so little, say,*
*Couldst Thou talk Thy Father's way?—*

# Helen Keller's "First" Christmas

*The excitement of Christmas, for a child, does
not depend on eyes and ears alone, as Helen
Keller shows in this childhood recollection.*

The first Christmas after Miss Sullivan came to Tuscumbia was a great event. . . . Christmas Eve, after I had hung my stocking, I lay awake a long time, pretending to be asleep and keeping alert to see what Santa Claus would do when he came. At last I fell asleep with a new doll and a white bear in my arms. Next morning it was I who waked the whole family with my first "Merry Christmas!" I found surprises, not in the stocking only, but on the table, on all the chairs, at the door, on the very window-sill; indeed, I could hardly walk without stumbling on a bit of Christmas wrapped up in tissue paper. But when my teacher presented me with a canary, my cup of happiness overflowed.

Little Tim was so tame that he would hop on my finger and eat candied cherries out of my hand. Miss Sullivan taught me to take all the care of my new pet. Every morning after breakfast I prepared his bath, made his cage clean and sweet, filled his cups with fresh seed and water from the well-house, and hung a spray of chickweed in his swing.

One morning I left the cage on the window-seat while I went to fetch water for his bath. When I returned I felt a big cat brush past me as I opened the door. At first I did not realize what had happened; but when I put my hand in the cage and Tim's pretty wings did not meet my touch or his small pointed claws take hold of my finger, I knew that I should never see my sweet little singer again.

## Oranges and Lemons

Oran- ges and lem- ons, Say the

bells of St. Cle- ments; You owe me five

farth ings, Say the bells of St. Mar- tin's.

When will you pay me, Say the Bells of Old Bailey;
When I grow rich, Say the bells of Shoreditch.

When will that be? Say the bells of Stepney;
I'm sure I don't know, Says the Great Bell of Bow.

## Nuts in May

Here we go gath- er- ing Nuts in May,

Nuts in May, Nuts in May, Here we go gathering

Nuts in May, On a cold and fros- ty morn- ing.

Who will you have for Nuts in May, Nuts in May, Nuts in May
Who will you have for Nuts in May, On a cold and frosty morning?

We'll have (Tommy) for Nuts in May, Nuts in May, Nuts in May,
We'll have (Tommy) for Nuts in May, On a cold and frosty morning.

## Patapan

*The word "carol" stems from the Old French "carole,"*
*which first meant a round dance accompanied by singing.*
*This Burgundian "noël," believed to have been written in*
*the 17th Century, shows the joyous spirit of the early carols.*

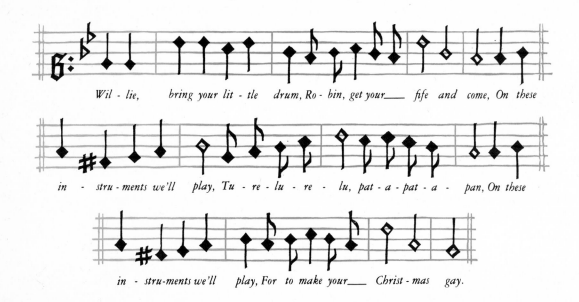

Wil - lie, bring your lit - tle drum, Ro - bin, get your___ fife and come, On these

in - stru- ments we'll play, Tu - re- lu - re - lu, pat - a - pat - a - pan, On these

in - stru- ments we'll play, For to make your___ Christ - mas gay.

# IV

# CHRISTMAS, TIME OF MAGIC

THIS IS MEETING-AGAIN TIME. Home is the magnet. The winter land roars and hums with the eager speed of return journeys. The dark is noisy and bright with late-night arrivals—doors thrown open, running shadows on snow, open arms, kisses, voices and laughter, laughter at everything and nothing. Inarticulate, giddying and confused are those original minutes of being back again. The very familiarity of everything acts like shock. Contentment has to be drawn in slowly, steadyingly, in deep breaths—there is so much of it. We rely on home not to change, and it does not, wherefore we give thanks. Again Christmas: abiding point of return. Set apart by its mystery, mood and magic, the season seems in a way to stand outside time. All that is dear, that is lasting, renews its hold on us: we are home again.

"HOME FOR CHRISTMAS," ELIZABETH BOWEN

A SPLENDID BLAZE *of many-colored lights outlines a country house (opposite) and casts its magical radiance on the wintry night.*

# A SEASON OF MUSIC AND WONDERMENT

A VISIT TO SANTA *is a vital part of every American child's Christmas, though some small visitors are overwhelmed with awe.*

THE MAGIC OF CHRISTMAS is a powerful magic indeed. It transforms ordinary city streets into fanciful avenues of multicolored lights, it inspires the tone-deaf to join in merry carols, it can soften the heart of a Scrooge. Christmas magic reunites scattered families, causes perfect strangers to greet one another and fills up the churches. And the magic continues to work, season after season.

"Miracles happen only to those who believe in them," says an old French proverb. At Christmastime people enjoy being credulous. The very atmosphere tingles with anticipation of wishes that might come true. At Christmas, man recaptures some of the lighthearted faith of childhood, when it was easy to believe in Santa driving his reindeer across the skies, when it was even possible to hear (if one listened closely) the faint jingle of his sleigh bells in that endless night of waiting for Christmas Day to dawn.

For this is a time of anticipation. Excitement builds as each new sign of Christmas appears. Store windows are decorated, spruce and fir trees make forests of parking lots, Salvation Army bands play carols on street corners, the community tree glows on the courthouse lawn or village green. In schools and churches rehearsals begin for Nativity plays and oratorios. In homes, Christmas cards are addressed, parties planned, cookies decorated. As Christmas Day draws nearer, it seems that almost everyone is waiting for something—for the snow to fall, for the arrival of the exciting annual package from relatives far away, for the thrill of bringing home the Christmas tree and rediscovering, in the attic or hall closet, beloved ornaments from Christmases past.

Now is the time when children reveal their impossible desires. Little girls are not afraid to ask for ponies, little boys dream of space ships that will really fly to the moon. Even sensible adults are caught up in the spirit of what-might-be. A vision of perfect family happiness is part of the season, and they plunge willingly into all sorts of preparations and plans in order to give this priceless gift on Christmas Day.

The aura of mystery and magic that surrounds Christmas is due in part to the many legends that have grown up around this important celebration. If animals can talk on Christmas Eve, if cows kneel down in their stalls and bees hum psalms, then might not other miraculous events take place?

So the sense of excitement grows until Christmas morning dawns at last, making clear what all the preparation and waiting meant. The miracle has happened after all: it is the birth of Christ, which took place nearly 2,000 years ago, but still happens in the hearts of men every Christmas of every year.

"The age of miracles past?" wrote Thomas Carlyle. "The age of miracles is forever here!" Faith in miracles is the true magic of Christmas.

A FAMILIAR SIGHT *at Christmastime is a Salvation Army bandsman (above) playing carols in the streets. The cheerful strains of "Hark! The Herald Angels Sing" or "The First Nowell," though sometimes off key, inspire busy shoppers to think of others at this season of giving, drop a coin or two in the pot, and go their ways whistling or singing with the fading trumpets and tubas.*

A TASSELLED HORSE *draws a sleigh full of revelers (above). "Hear the sledges with the bells*
*—Silver bells!" Edgar Allan Poe wrote. "What a world of merriment their melody foretells!"*

104

# A
# DAZZLE
# OF SNOW

There is little reason to believe that there was snow in Bethlehem on that first Christmas. Yet snow and Christmas have long been associated. When Good King Wenceslaus looked out on St. Stephen's Day, "the snow lay round about." In some Scandinavian countries, people still ride in sleighs or ski to pre-dawn Christmas services. In this country, snow at Christmas is a tradition; even in the Southern states, Santa is supposed to travel by sleigh, and artificial snow and icicles glitter on the Christmas trees, though the grass may be green outside.

Certainly a fresh, soft snowfall adds to the magic of Christmas, and the most splendid skyrockets and Roman candles set off by Southern children can hardly compensate for the joys of snow.

Wherever snow falls, it changes the lives of those who live there. It brings them the particular beauty of the wintry landscape, the pleasure of hearing snow creak underfoot, and a deep need for the shelter of home. Houses smell of wet mittens and ski-wax as well as of roast turkey, and children can scarcely wait until Christmas dinner is over to rush out into the cold to try out new sleds on the steepest slopes of all.

FOUR HAPPY BOYS *and a dog that got left behind (below) race down a snowy hill. Toboggans, adapted from the bark-and-skin sleds of the Algonquian, provide fun—and thrilling spills.*

# SYMBOLS
# OF THE
# CHRISTMAS
# SPIRIT

Christmas is a time of merriment; it is also a time for reverence. On Christmas Eve, many churches in brilliantly lighted cities and quiet towns hold midnight services to celebrate, with rich ceremony, the humble birth of Jesus.

Merriment and reverence are by no means mutually exclusive. The affectionate worship of Christ as the Babe of Bethlehem, born in humility, was especially stressed by St. Francis of Assisi. St. Francis is associated with Christmas because of his popularization of the crèche, described in Volume Two, and his great love of the simple religious songs which were forerunners of the Christmas carol. He once advised a Brother to mix singing with his preaching—"for what are the servants of God if not His minstrels, who ought to stir and incite the hearts of men to spiritual joy?"

St. Francis' celebration of Christmas in Greccio in 1223 was humble indeed compared with the Christmases of today, which partake of customs developed through 2,000 years in many lands. But all Christmas customs, whether rooted in pagan festivals, folklore or church rituals, express that "spiritual joy" of which St. Francis spoke—a joy which we glory in manifesting during the magical season of Christmas.

*"CROSSES ARE LADDERS that lead to heaven," says an old English proverb. At Christmas the lofty symbol (above) rises dramatically over the secular city, lifting the hearts of those below.*

*ST. FRANCIS OF ASSISI is one of the most loved of all saints (opposite). A gay youth until he renounced his ways, he never lost his love of songs, of people, and of the simple joys of life.*

106

## IN THIS VOLUME
## ANTHOLOGY SELECTIONS

## CHRISTMAS MUSIC

# INDEX

*This symbol preceding a page number indicates a photograph or painting of the subject mentioned.

# PICTURE CREDITS

*Credits for pictures from left to right are separated by commas, from top to bottom by dashes. In the case of original designs, the photographer's name appears in parentheses—e.g., (Herbert Orth).*

# FOR FURTHER READING

Anglund, Joan Walsh, *Christmas Is a Time of Giving.* Harcourt, Brace & World, 1961.

Ballam, Harry, and Phyllis Digby Morton, *The Christmas Book.* Sampson Low, N.D.

Becker, May Lamberton, ed., *The Home Book of Christmas.* Dodd, Mead & Company, 1960.

Church, Francis P., *Is There a Santa Claus?* Grosset & Dunlap, 1938.

Davies, Valentine, *Miracle on 34th Street.* Harcourt, Brace & Co., 1947.

Eliot, T. S., *The Cultivation of Christmas Trees.* Farrar, Straus and Cudahy, 1956.

Field, Eugene, *Christmas Tales and Christmas Verse.* Scribner, 1912.

Frost, Lesley, ed., *Come Christmas.* Coward McCann, Inc., 1929.

Ghéon, Henri, *The Journey of the Three Kings.* Sheed and Ward Inc., 1935.

Grahame, Kenneth, *Bertie's Escapade.* J. B. Lippincott, 1949.

Gunnarsson, Gunnar, *The Good Shepherd.* The Bobbs-Merrill Company, 1940.

Karasz, Ilonka (pictures), *The Twelve Days of Christmas.* Harper & Brothers, 1949.

McGinley, Phyllis, *Merry Christmas, Happy New Year.* Viking Press, 1958; *Mince Pie and Mistletoe.* J. B. Lippincott Company, 1961.

Morris, Harrison S., *In the Yule-Log Glow.* 4 vols., J. B. Lippincott, 1892.

Posselt, E., ed., *The World's Greatest Christmas Stories.* Prentice-Hall, 1950.

Sayers, Dorothy L., *The Days of Christ's Coming.* London, Hamish Hamilton, 1960.

Schmauch, Walter W., *Christmas Literature through the Centuries.* Walter M. Hill, 1938.

Smith, Lillian, *Memory of a Large Christmas.* W. W. Norton, 1962.

Thomas, Dylan, *A Child's Christmas in Wales.* New Directions, 1954.

Todd, Marion R., *The Christmas Book.* The William-Frederick Press, 1959.

Undset, Sigrid, *Christmas and Twelfth Night.* Longmans, Green & Co., 1932.

Van Dyke, Henry, *The Spirit of Christmas.* Charles Scribner's Sons, 1957.

Wilson, Dorothy, ed., *The Family Christmas Book.* Prentice-Hall, 1957.

# ACKNOWLEDGMENTS

The editors of this volume are indebted to Grace Manney, home economist, for the preparation and testing of recipes, to Paula Peck for the sweet bread recipes and to Linda Wolfe for advice on the selection of foods; to Dr. Richard Kraus, Teachers College, Columbia University, and to John Peter Associates for advice on Christmas entertainment for children; to Byron Dobell, who initiated the project and saw it through its earliest stages, and to Daniel Longwell, former Chairman of the Board of Editors of LIFE; to Brother William J. Kiefer, S. M., Randolph E. Haugan, Bernice Leary, Margaret Reynolds and John Hadfield for generously making available the results of their extensive studies of Christmas literature; and to the many other individuals who contributed valuable assistance.

*Production Staff for Time Incorporated*
*Arthur J. Murphy Jr. (Vice President and Director of Production)*
*Robert E. Foy, James P. Menton and Caroline Ferri*
*Body text photocomposed under the direction of*
*Albert J. Dunn and Arthur J. Dunn*

✕